UP NORTH
DOWN SOUTH

➤ *a memoir* ◆

My classmate 1953
Black River High School!

JOHN ALAN BARNARD

(I was class treasurer)

ISBN: 978-1-7351535-0-6

Edited by Susan Edwards
Book design by David Provolo

Cover photo: The author and his bride, Sylvia.
Back cover photo: The author's childhood home.

To my Sylvia,
for 60 years plus we shared life together,
sharing all the moments, whatever they might be
we did it together, and to lose her was devastating.
I miss her so much.

CONTENTS

PREFACE

On November 18, 2019, I reached my eighty-fourth birthday. I have learned to be a caregiver, which was the hardest thing I had ever done.

My wife passed away on October 23, 2018 after a lengthy illness and a terrible time for all of us. I decided that I needed to do something to keep myself busy. Several years ago someone suggested to me that I write a book. Well I started taking notes over the years and labeled my book *Up North Down South*. I kept a file.

As I began to research the notes, I soon found that the book was not what I was going to do. I had so many different things happen to me over the years that I decided a memoir was the best approach. So I got started, and with the help of the Geek Squad I was able to purchase two nice HP computers and an HP printer with a lot of instructions. I also got software called The Dragon.

I dictated all these thoughts into the computer after writing them down on a yellow pad. I had no punctuation and no idea of how to go about it. So now I have had to rewrite everything. I did try to punctuate it and correct as I went along. I will continue after I have the new version edited and manuscript to add to the material. I hope someone will find this interesting and enjoy reading the incidents that occurred during my eighty-three years.

— PART 1 —
CHILDHOOD

CHAPTER 1

Life at 66 Main Street, Ludlow, Vermont

November 18, 1935

It's snowing, blowing, freezing, cold as hell. Call Dr. Carey and hurry up. Margaret is in the upstairs bedroom about to deliver her baby.

John Allan Barnard has arrived. A healthy baby boy eight pounds, six ounces and twenty-two inches long, and the mother is doing just fine. The first grandson of Maggie and Clarence Davis is born.

Being born in the upstairs bedroom at 66 Main St. had a great significance in my early life, and for the next nineteen years, this was my home. The stories that happened during these nineteen years as best I can remember are reflected in the following memories.

My Uncle John nicknamed me Babe. My mother worked and lived away from 66 Main St. most of my young life. My grandparents, Maggie and Clarence Davis, and their sons Uncle John and Uncle Justin were my real family during this time.

My earliest memory is of the sand pile Uncle John had fixed for me in the back of the driveway where my grandmother could watch me through the kitchen window. I wore a harness attached to a guidewire running most of the way down the driveway, which kept me from getting into the street so my grandmother did not have to watch over me the all the time.

Uncle John had always given me plenty of toys to play with, soldiers and forts. When I was older he used to buy me a lot of Tonka toys which were really neat. I had a pet dog named Chang. He was a chow and very protective of me. He watched over me all the time I was out in the yard playing in the sand pile.

The author at age 5 at 66 Main Street,
Ludlow, Vermont.

I had a little neighbor friend whose name was Bissonnette and who lived across the street from me. She used to play with me and my toys in the sand pile. One day she started to leave and the dog would not let her go, he would grab her pants with his teeth and pull her back to keep her from leaving the yard. She really got scared and started crying. My grandmother came out and took care of the issue. I had to give the dog back to my Grandma Barnard in Woodstock, Vermont. I surely did miss him.

The next thing I remember is the big clock on the mantelpiece in the living room. It had two keys Grandpa used to wind it every night. One of the keys was for the weights and the other for the springs. I still have this clock in my possession now.

Grandpa smoked a pipe and he used Prince Albert tobacco. He would hold me in his lap at night in front of the fireplace and when I had an earache he would blow that warm smoke into my ear until I fell asleep.

The downstairs at 66 Main St. had a kitchen, dining room and large living room. At the end of the living room was a large glass panel door that led into the hallway. I used to wear pajamas that had the feet built into them. The dining room and the living room both had hardwood floors. I could start in the kitchen and slide through the dining room and into the living room on those hardwood floor and stop just short of the glass door.

My grandmother had warned me not to do that as I would get hurt someday, so when she was out of sight I would occasionally slide all the way to the living room. One day, she was in the outer shed and could not see me or hear me, so I took a chance. I slid all the way to the living room and crashed into the glass door.

I started crying and she rushed to my aid and carried me to the kitchen and set me on the kitchen sink. Turning on the cold water, she started picking the glass out of my arms and face. I wasn't really hurt bad, but I got cut up with the glass pretty bad. She cleaned me up and my sliding days were over. I healed up very quickly.

The kitchen table was large with high-back benches on both sides. On one end was a radiator, which was my seat and had to be covered with an asbestos cover to keep my butt from being burned. Grandpa would sit in the big chair and my job was to make sure his water glass did not get empty. He would drink three or four glasses of water at every meal so I kept a sharp lookout to make sure he had plenty of fresh water.

In the kitchen was a big wood box. My job was to keep that wood box full of small kindling wood so my grandmother could keep the stove hot. I would have to go down to the cellar and usually chop up kindling before bringing it to the wood box. I would also have to bring larger chunks to put by the fireplace to keep us warm in the winter.

The cellar was large and could hold a lot of wood. We would have to fill it up about half full so we would have wood all winter long. This was a weekend project that required all hands on deck. Grandpa had pulpwood placed in the driveway on Friday, and on Saturday, he would drive the Chrysler out to the driveway, jack up the back end and remove the tire, leaving the rim. He had a large belt which he would put around the rim and stretch it to a bench he had made especially for cutting pulpwood into chunks. He would then start the old Chrysler up, attach the belt to the wheel rim, connect it to the saw, and away we would go.

The stronger boys would put the pulpwood on the bench saw and Grandpa would cut the chunks, then they would pass the chunks through the window of the cellar to me, and I would stack them up as high as I could so we would have plenty of wood for the winter. This would take all day Saturday and most of Sunday.

The rest of the cellar consisted of a potato room, which was dark and had a large table where Grandma kept the potatoes. Next to the potato bin was a shelf where she kept her pickles and other canned stuff where it was cool in the wintertime. Uncle Justin decided later on to put a shower in the basement and it was dangerous because he didn't have a lot of safety precautions with electric wires but it was convenient. I took a lot of showers down there but had to be very cautious.

There was also a huge furnace that heated the whole house in wintertime. The house was full of radiators and burned fuel oil. Mr. Martel and the Sunoco truck would come and fill up the tank as often as needed. When the furnace would go full blast you could hear the radiators pinging and popping.

The kitchen had a refrigerator on the left-hand side with drawers underneath, and this is where Grandpa kept his Crowley's cheese and hard cider. On Sunday evening Grandpa and his friends would have plenty of hard cider and cheese, and tell wild stories. I used to really enjoy listening to them.

There was a countertop next to the refrigerator where Grandma kept her pies. You could always get a good piece of apple pie and some good Crowley's cheese and a good glass of hard cider. There were two sinks made of slate and another counter with three drawers. The bottom drawer contained materials for polishing shoes. The other two held different kitchen utensils.

The most significant thing in the kitchen was an eight-by-twelve-inch mirror Grandma had put up on the wall and tilted toward you when you stood in front of it. This was called the inspection. Before leaving for school every morning she would stand in front of the mirror and check me over to see I had no dirty spots on my face or behind my ears and if I did, give me a small spit bath. She always kept a handkerchief close at hand. It also served as a good reminder when you left the house to check your personal appearance.

The Back Porch

The back porch was a large L-shaped porch covered with grapevines and a railing all around. Grandma and Grandpa used to sit on the back porch, weather permitting, and visit a lot. The extreme back was the L-shape and it had two big beds. This is where I slept most of the time. In the wintertime I used to have to pull a canvas over the top of my covers to keep the snow off my quilts. It was a small distance to the kitchen back door, and in the winter I would have to make a beeline for the kitchen door to keep from freezing.

Grandma would stick her head out the back door and call me say, "Babe, breakfast is ready." And I would scamper as fast as I could to get inside. Sleeping on the back porch had a distinct advantage to me is I could slip out over the railing anytime I wished and no one would miss me. I confess I did this several times, probably to meet some young lady who was sneaking out also.

Making Hard Cider

The front cellar was mostly empty of clutter and had a concrete floor. This is where we made our hard cider. Fifteen to twenty big barrels of pressed apples filled with brown sugar and raisins. When the fermentation began, you could hear the bubbling all over the cellar. We had a special kind of hard cider that we called champagne cider. This was made with distilled water and a siphon hose running from the distilled water container sealed with wax into the barrel that was also sealed with wax. This particular cider would have an extra kick to it. We always had a good supply of it.

The Workshop

Grandpa, being a carpenter by trade, had a large workshop full of all the tools of the trade. At the north end of the workshop was a schoolhouse stove that kept the whole workshop warm in the wintertime because it burned large chunks of wood all day. At the opposite end of the shop was a small room with a closed door on one side and an opening on the backside. He kept a milk cow there most of the time, which provided us with fresh milk. Further down the yard about two dozen chickens were in a fenced yard with a chicken coop, so we had plenty of eggs and chickens to eat.

Storm Windows

66 Main St. was a twenty-room house with three stories. To protect the house in winter time, storm windows had to be put on all the windows in the house. This was a major undertaking. The windows were stored in the cellar and had to be taken out and washed. They were placed over the regular windows and each storm window had a set of six screws, two in the top, two in the middle, and two in the bottom.

You needed a large ladder to reach the windows on top of the house. Someone had to climb the ladder, someone had to hoist the window, and someone had to hold it while it was being attached. There were no automatic screwdrivers in those days, so it took someone who could sustain hanging windows and screwing them to the house.

They were very efficient and kept the cold and storm from damaging the house. They had to come down in the spring and be stored all summer until the whole process had to be done again. This was a major project.

Strange Sickness

When I was about seven or eight years old I became very ill. I would have these terrific nosebleeds that were very hard to stop. I would have horrible headaches, nausea, and fever. The doctor decided to put me in the hospital because he had no idea what was wrong with me. They took me to Rutland Hospital and isolated me in some area of the hospital. They ran several tests, and didn't really want to get too close to me. They would not let me have any visitors, no family, only nurses and doctors.

My grandmother finally came to the hospital, marched herself right back to my room and took one look at me and my surroundings and said, "Get dressed, we're going home." With no discharge and no conversation, she marched me right out of the hospital and into the car and they drove me home. She put me in the bed, called Dr. Carey and he came over and checked me out. For several days I stayed in the bed with only liquids.

After while I began to get my strength back and in several weeks I was over that. Dr. Carey told my grandmother that he thought I had mononucleosis. I never had any more trouble and was glad of that.

The Adoption

Grandma and Grandpa Davis had good friends who lived in Connecticut; their names were Elsie and Carl Pason. Carl was an executive for the GE Corporation and had a cottage on a lake. They had been friends with my grandmother and grandfather for years. They had taken quite a shine to me.

My mother at this time was not at home, and my grandmother and grandfather were raising me. Their friends had no children and knew that my grandmother and grandfather were going to raise me. The Pasons said they would like to adopt me.

My grandparents' response was gentle but firm, that they would raise me. This was the only time the subject was ever brought up and was never discussed again. They remained friends for a long time.

Killing Chickens

I had watched my grandfather pick out chickens for cooking. He would take out two at a time. He had a pole about five feet long and round like a cane. He would walk into the chicken yard and whack a couple on the head and then we would butcher and pluck them to get them ready for Grandma's cooking.

This looked pretty easy to me, so I decided one day to pick a couple of them. I got the pole. But I didn't stop with two. I whacked four or five. I didn't know how to butcher them so I just left them in the yard.

Grandpa came home that night and did his chores. He spotted the chickens. I knew my goose was cooked. He called to me from the backyard to come down to the chicken coop. When I did, he confronted me about the dead chickens and I told him what happened.

He didn't get mad, which was his nature; he just told me that I would be responsible for plucking, butchering, and preparing the chickens for Grandmother to cook, and that I wasn't allowed in the chick yard anymore.

The First Whirlpool

My grandmother had been a teacher in Boston, Massachusetts, when she was younger. She would tell me how tired her feet were when she came home at night from walking on the cobblestone streets. She said she would put them in the commode and pull the chain and the cool water swirling around in the commode would give her some relaxation. She didn't know it but that was the beginning of the whirlpool.

Jumping Jack

Grandpa had put together a sled he called the Jumping Jack. It had one runner, made from a curved barrel stave, and one seat. The seat was one single board about two inches wide and twenty-four inches long. It was a great challenge to try to ride the Jumping Jack down the mountain. It was really fun when we had a fresh snow and started at the top.

You would have nothing to hang on to but the board that you

were sitting on. Your feet were placed on the runner, and off you would go. The only way to steer this thing was with body motion and pulling on the seat and turning. I don't think any of us really mastered the jumping Jack. But we had a whole lot of fun trying.

Basketball Outdoors

Grandpa had built me a nice backboard with a rim. He mounted it on a tree exactly ten feet off the ground. Day after day, I played basketball by myself shooting and dribbling. Since I had no brothers or sisters, I had to entertain myself. As I look back now, I wish I had paid more attention to learning some of the trade that my grandfather was so good at. I didn't do it but hindsight is always better. Rain or shine snow or sleet I played just about every day with the basketball.

Why I Like Waldorf Salad

My mother married Patrick Stryhas, and they moved into the upstairs apartment at 66 Main St. I had a bedroom in the back of the apartment. Mother had fixed a big supper one night with a roast and all the fixings.

About halfway through the supper she started having severe labor pains and was rushed to the hospital. There was no one else left at the house with me, so my job was to clean up the kitchen and do the dishes.

She had made a big bowl of Waldorf salad which I had never had before, and while cleaning up I kept eating from the bowl until it was all gone. Boy, was it delicious. It had dates and apples and everything in it, and to this day I still like it very much. That night my sister Peggy was born, and I became a big fan of Waldorf salad.

Aunt Becky

My mother's sister, Aunt Becky, died at an early age while being operated on in the hospital. She had married a man named Robert

Wilson. He was a reporter for the Associated Press. He was sent overseas and was captured by the Germans and imprisoned at a camp called Stalag 22. When the war was over, he would come to the house to visit.

He only spoke about his captivity one time. It was terrible, and he later went on to become an outstanding reporter for AP. Incidentally sometime later a movie was made starring William Holden about Stalag 17 so it must've been pretty much a true story.

Music Lessons

Both my mother and grandmother were determined for me to have some sort of musical background. They started with the violin, which I did not respond to well. The clarinet had the same results. Then came the piano. My mother was very good at the piano and had a great voice. My music teacher used to come to the house for one hour every week to teach me. His name was Napoleon Ianni. No kidding. He was a high school band director and a very good musician in his own right. He had a great orchestra that played on the weekends at the Lake Coolidge dances on Saturday night.

He would give me assignments for the next lesson and tell me to practice. When he arrived he was all business. He would stand behind the back of the piano bench and say, "Okay, let's get started." He would then get a good hold on my right ear, and every time I made a mistake, my ear would get a twist. My grandmother used to say to me, "I don't have to see if your lessons are okay. I just need to check your ear for redness."

After three years of piano, I switched to the trumpet and became very good at it and I really enjoyed it. I played in the high school band and was second trumpet. I continued to play the trumpet until I had my teeth removed as a result of chemotherapy and radiation. Even with dentures I could not put any pressure on my lips so my trumpet is still in the case.

Grandpa and His Hammer

We were doing some work on his workshop outside putting some fascia boards on the shop. This was long before he ever had his accident, which I will detail later, and he could do most anything at that time. I would stand on the ground and hand him the board, and he would nail it to the rafters. There came a time when he could no longer hold the nail with his hand and hammer. I watched him with amazement and learned something brand-new.

He would take one eight-penny nail at a time, lodge it in the claws of the hammer and without looking up he would swing his hammer with the nail in the claw and drive it into the board. He would then proceed to pound in the nail without ever looking upward never missing a lick I guess that came with practice over the years.

Grandpa could do most anything with his hands. Over the years he had made my mother a four-poster black cherry wood bed that would be considered a king-size bed today. He started out from scratch with a big chunk of black cherry wood and turned the whole thing out on his lathe by hand. He had given Margaret and Pat (my stepfather) this bed as a wedding present. My brother Bruce said the bed is still in existence and is located in Connecticut where my sister passed away. Several years later, Grandpa handcrafted a beautiful gun cabinet for Pat. And Bruce said he has that gun cabinet today too.

Raccoon Hunting

Pat used to love to hunt raccoon and always kept him a few dogs. I used to love to go with him and all of his friends because it was exciting to listen to the dogs trail the coons, and listen to the different tones of the barks when they picked up the scent. When they follow the scent there would be short bursts of barking. This could go on for some time and we would follow the noise.

Suddenly the tone of the barks would change. It would be a howling and that would mean the raccoon was treed. That's when the excitement began. We would get to the tree and the dogs would be clawing the bottom of it, letting us know that raccoon was up in the tree. Most of the time someone would crawl up the tree and shake the raccoon out.

The coon would hit the ground with a thud and try to get away from the dogs. Sometimes they could and sometimes they couldn't. You could shine a large three-cell or four-cell flashlight into the tree and see the eyes of the raccoon. Once in a while, the tree was too large to climb up and shake the raccoon out. Then they would shoot the raccoon from the ground. The dogs were put on the leash when this occurred.

One night, when we were coon hunting Pat said, "Okay, Babe, it's your turn to shake him out. This was my first time, and I was a little bit nervous. But I climbed up the tree until I came to the branch the raccoon was sitting on. I had on heavy clothes and climbed out as far as I could and got ahold of the tree limb. The raccoon was snarling and raising hell. I shook and shook and shook and shook finally raccoon dropped on hard and hit the ground. I climbed back down, and Pat said. "Good job, Babe."

Occasionally we would be able to catch some baby raccoons, and Pat would take them home in a cage. I used to sit and watch them eat their food and how they would wash everything. These were exciting things for me to do when I was a child. I never forget that.

Finding Gold

The Boy Scouts had a summer camp on Lake Plymouth. One summer, when we were camping there, we discovered the prospector. He had a small cold cream jar and in it he had some gold flakes. This was the first time I had ever seen any gold and it was quite fascinating. He had been panning along the creek for some time. And at that time, if I remember, our leader said gold was selling for $32 an ounce while today's market lists it $1,514.89 per ounce. Not too bad an investment.

19

My Great-Grandfather Moses Townsend

My grandmother's father, Moses Townsend, was very tall thin and had a large gray beard. He lived in the stone house across from the library on Main Street in Ludlow, Vermont. The house was always dark and cold inside. The only furniture I remember was in the kitchen; it consisted of a very simple big wooden table and four chairs.

I remember watching Moses Townsend eating his English peas with a knife. He would roll them down his beard and into his mouth and never drop one. I understand that this is an English custom.

Mr. Townsend had a hankering for horehound candy. He would send me to the drugstore to pick him up a bag of candy from time to time. They look like cough drops and have a licorice taste. He would always have one underneath his lower lip, which kinda looked like he was dipping snuff.

Mr. Townsend would make his presence known in a big way on Christmas Eve. It would be up at the house of his daughter, Zoa Fletcher, who was Grandma's sister. He would sit in the big chair and pull out this large cloth bag where he kept his cash. He would motion to you to come sit in his lap. He then would reach in this big cloth bag, pull out a wad of rolled up cash and pull some money out and give it to you and you would hug his neck.

As a great-grandson I received a five-dollar bill. The closer you got to being his daughters, the rate went up. Each of his four daughters got a fifty-dollar bill. This was his way of giving Christmas presents.

He was a very shrewd businessman and had acquired a great deal of land prior to his death. He was a good father and encouraged all the children to get an education and to do well. One particular parcel of land that he owned was around Lake Ninevah. (I will discuss this later on in great detail.) He died January 17, 1945.

The Cannon

Grandpa had a cannon that he had acquired over the years and it was called a yacht cannon. It was made of solid mahogany wheels, brass cotter pins and a mahogany frame. It had a solid brass barrel with a breach and a lanyard.

On July 4 he would roll it out to the street and we would have to stop traffic both ways for about 500 yards. He would lower the wad in the powder and pull the lanyard. The recoil would send the cannon shooting backwards for several feet and make one hell of a racket. This was something I really looked forward to every Fourth of July. It was exciting.

My younger brother Bruce has this cannon in his possession at this time. I hope I might be able to get my hands on it so I can give it to my children. It has many memories and I only have two other items from Grandma and Grandpa, a clock and a walrus tusk.

My Injured Collie

I had rescued this beautiful collie dog from the highway that had been struck by a car and was lying in the snow on the side of Route 103. I picked her up and took her to the back shed in the garage and cared for her for several days. She didn't have any broken bones but she was bruised pretty bad.

After about eight days, she was able to stand up and get around, so at the end of two weeks she was being pretty feisty. It was winter time and there was plenty of snow outside. How she loved to romp in the deep snow.

We became inseparable and had a great time together. I would take her upstairs to the bedroom where I stayed and crack the window so she could have fresh air when I went off to school. One day she was looking out the window and saw me across the street. One of those windows was open and she got out on the roof. She was running back and forth wanting to come to me. She finally jumped off into the snow and came running across the road to me. I had to take her and put her up in the shed so I could get off to school.

One day she managed to get the door open to the rest of the apartment and wandered into the kitchen where mother had cooked a big roast and was cooling it on the stove. She proceeded to get the roast down and eat the whole thing and that was the end of her being able to stay in the house. I had to put her back in the shed and eventually had to give her away to a little girl who lived in the country. I checked on her from time to time and she was real happy and so was the little girl.

The Knoll

Across the street from 66 Main St. is where the Sargent family lived. Gary Sargent had been Attorney General of the United States when Calvin Coolidge was president. He was a big man and smoked a corncob pipe all the time. I did have a picture of me at three months of age being held by Gary Sargent smoking his pipe, but Hurricane Katrina ruined most of my pictures of the early days in Vermont.

Behind the Sargent house was a very large hill that was fenced in at the bottom with fence wire, not barbed wire. The hill was steep and would crust over in the winter with solid ice. The bottom of the hill had a large gate that kept the cows in during the summer and was open in the winter.

One of our favorite sports was to strap creepers (spiked soles for walking on ice) onto our boots and climb to the top of the hill with a piece of cardboard. We would jump onto the cardboard and slide down the hill lickety-split trying to hit the opening in the gate.

More likely, we would crash into the fence. Having heavy clothing on protected us from dangerous injury. Sometimes when we hit the opening of the gate we could slide almost up to the backyard of the Sargents' house. This was a great thrill and very hard to do.

Grandpa's Whipping

I had a friend named Charlie Proor. He lived across the bridge on Pleasant Street and we used to play together quite a bit. We used to go behind the Sargents' place in the mountains and just roam around and have a good time. One day we ran across some construction where they were building a new road. It must've been on Saturday because there was nobody about and we looked everything over pretty good.

Upon a ledge were several boxes, so we got one of them down. They were big boxes but we opened them up and they looked like they had casings inside. So we each grabbed a handful, put them in our pockets, and headed home.

That night at the supper table after I had finished eating, I reached in my pocket and pulled one of these casings out, they were soft enough to chew and they would bend a little bit. Grandpa asked me what I had.

I said, "I don't know; we found them up in the area where they're building a new road."

He said, "You got any more?"

I jingled in my pockets and said there were several in there.

He said, "Let's put them all on the table and tell me if Charlie has any of these in his possession."

I said, "Oh yeah, he grabbed a handful just like I did."

Grandpa said, "We're going to load up and go over to Charlie's house and see how many he has got."

I didn't understand why but I knew better than to question his judgment. So we went to Charlie's house, and Grandpa knocked on the door. Charlie's mother came to the door and Grandpa identified himself and asked if Charlie was home.

She said, "Yes, he is in the back." She called him and he came to the front. Charlie did not have a daddy, and his mother was raising him the best she could.

Grandpa asked Charlie about the casings and Charlie told him just like I did and he had several of him. When Grandpa told him to go get them and bring them out, he did. He then told Charlie and me to get in the truck and we also complied. He then explained to Charlie's mother what these casings were. She was terrified.

We had got ahold of some dynamite caps and didn't know it. On the way home, Grandpa stopped the truck on the Black River bridge.

23

He threw all the casings in the water, which is pretty deep, and then we drove on to the house.

We all went to the back porch where he had a big rocking chair. He then told us what we had done and how dangerous it could have been for everybody concerned. He then put me across his knee and proceeded to give me a good whipping. He was not gentle about it either. He did likewise to Charlie, and then drove him home. This was the only whipping I ever got from my grandfather. He never lost his temper, which was his way; he was always gentle.

Bow and Arrow

My friend Charlie Proor and I were playing cowboys and Indians behind the Sargents' house. My Uncle Justin had gotten ahold of some metal tips kinda shaped like bullets that would fit over the ends of arrows. I had gotten a bow and arrows for Christmas and was just waiting for the weather to warm up so I could try it out. Charlie had two toy guns. I had managed to put some of these tips on my arrows and they were pretty sharp.

I was hiding, waiting for Charlie to show his face. When he did, I let go with one of those arrows and struck him in the side of the head. Down the bank he went, and I was scared to death. I ran home to get Grandma and I told her what had happened.

She arrived, tended to Charlie, and he was just scared to death. She wiped the blood away and he seemed to be okay but I wasn't allowed to play with the bow and arrow ever again because it was too dangerous.

Heidi Naess

Our next-door neighbors were the Naesses. They were from Scandinavia and the dad was a carpenter like my grandfather and they were the best of friends. He had a daughter named Heidi who was a couple years older than me.

One day Heidi and I were playing in the front cellar and I decided to try and kiss her. She unleashed such a severe kick to my groin that I almost passed out. She said, "Don't you ever try that again." I got the message loud and clear.

Several years later when we were alone up at Lake Rescue and out of college, she reminded me of her ability to kick in the right places and she and I both laughed.

I never did get to kiss Heidi.

Water Fights

Uncle John and Uncle Justin and my stepfather Pat were always pulling pranks on each other and me. Their favorite was to put a bucket of water over the door and leave the door open just a little bit and then tease you into chasing them.

While chasing them, you didn't pay much attention to the door and you would just open it and the water bucket would fall on your head. There would always be some kind of trap around the house to try to douse you with water and you had to be on the alert at all times.

Pat always wore a baseball cap outside, and would take it off and place it on the table in the kitchen. John figured out a way to really get back at him after Pat had gotten him and Justin several times. When Pat took his cap off and laid it on the table, John cracked about four eggs into his hat and then doused Pat with a bucket of water. He and Justin took off and Pat grabbed his hat from the table to chase them and threw it on his head and sure enough, eggs all over his face. That ended that episode.

Later on Pat decided he would get even with them, and he gathered about eight or ten eggs, stood at the back wall and waited for them to come out of the workshop. About halfway up the yard there was no protection for them and he let him have it. That was the end of that episode.

One day, I guess I had gotten John pretty bad. So they started to chase me. I ran up the front stairs and locked myself in the bathroom. They just sat down on the top stairs and waited for me to come out. I knew if I came out they would really give it to me bad so I just stayed there and waited.

There was a medicine cabinet in the bathroom, and it had a small enema bottle that would hold some water. So I filled it up with warm water and peeked through the keyhole and started taunting them. John stuck his eyeball right up front of the keyhole and I let him have a squirt with that enema bottle. They were furious, and Grandma had to rescue me from them that episode. We used to have some sort of devil stuff going on all the time but it was great fun.

Shoveling Snow

My job growing up was to keep the snow shoveled off the walkway and the driveway entrance. It also involved getting on the roof and chopping the ice from the overhang. This used to take a lot of time, and somehow I got tired of it.

It was the beginning of my seventh grade, and the doctor discovered I had a hernia. While I had it taken care of right away, it ended my snow shoveling for that winter. Uncle John had to take over the chores. He hated doing it, and I loved watching him do it. I used this as an excuse not to do any shoveling the whole winter. Boy it was nice. John didn't think so, but he never really did get that, and just did his job.

The Radio

In the dining room, we had a large upright radio. I think it was a Philco. On Sunday nights we would gather in the living room, Grandma, Grandpa, John, Justin, their friend Leon and I usually were the participants. We would listen to the radio, as there was no TV at this time.

The programs I would listen to that I can remember were *The Shadow* and *Inner Sanctum* I used to love the Bromo Seltzer commercial; it sounded like a freight train coming down the track. It would say, "Bromo Seltzer, Bromo Seltzer, Bromo Seltzer."

Grandma would always fix us a snack; usually we would pop some popcorn or have a big piece of apple pie with vanilla ice cream. This was the kind of spooky stuff we listened to back then.

Grandma's Boarder

Grandma's front room was rented to a boarder, a nice young fellow who worked uptown and carried his lunch pail with him every day. He had a serious problem though. When he was surprised by an unexpected sound, he would get startled and throw whatever he had in his hand in the direction the sound came from.

I'm sorry to say that I would hide behind a tree waiting for him to come home from work. When he got close enough to the tree, I would shout at him, and he would throw his lunch box in my direction. This was not a good thing to do. My grandmother found out about it and that was the end of it.

I did learn to play cards with him, and we often played. He taught me how to play cribbage, pitch, and High Low Jack.

Bitter Disappointment

My father Charlie was not mentioned very often, almost never, and only by my grandmother. She had told me he was not dependable person and not to pay much attention to his promises if he showed up.

One day close to Christmas time he did show up. He was a smaller man than I had imagined, and he had a gift of gab a mile long. He asked me what I liked to do. I told him I liked to ski. I had a new set of skis that were very good. I was good at skiing and my ski poles were old but solid.

He said, "Okay, I'll come pick you up tomorrow and take you to Claremont, New Hampshire, to the sporting goods store. And I'll buy you a new set of ski poles. How about that?"

I was excited. My grandmother was not in the room but she was close by. After my father had left, she took me to the kitchen table and sat me down. She told me not to be disappointed if he did not come back because he was not very dependable. I was so excited I didn't pay any attention to what she said. I could hardly sleep that night.

The next morning was Saturday, and I got all dressed up and stood in the bay window watching the snow fall, waiting for him to come. All day long I waited until finally it was dark. I was so hurt and disappointed that I cried myself to sleep that night.

I later vowed that when I got married and had children I would never, never, never disappoint them like that. I'm eighty-three years old now, and as I write this incident down, I still tear up knowing how bad a hurt it's left me with all my life, one that could not be undone. I would see my father four more times in his lifetime and I will note that later.

Opening the Sea Chest

When Grandpa was recuperating after his accident, which I will tell you about later, he stayed in the front bedroom in the bed most of the time. I spent a lot of time with him, just visiting. One day he sat up on the edge of the bed and said to me, "Let's open the old sea chest." I said okay.

This was truly an authentic sea chest with big rope handles and a big latch on the front. I pulled it up close to the bed, got me a chair, and sat down beside Grandpa. I sure was curious as to the contents.

When we got it open, it was full of old keepsakes. As we dug through some of them, we came across some envelopes, small ones that had clips attached to them. On the outside of these envelopes was writing. The name Bryant Chuck and Grinder was the factory where Grandpa had worked several years ago. These envelopes had been in the chest so long they were showing rusty spots. I handed him one of these envelopes. He took the gem clip off, and there was cash inside. These were all pay envelopes that he had just thrown in the chest and forgot about. There must've been eight or ten of them.

He said, "Babe, you'd better go get Maggie and show her these."

I did and when she came in, he handed her one of the envelopes and said, "I guess I just forgot to give you these."

She was happy to receive the cash and I was happy that I got to see inside the chest.

The Bull Moose Horn

The local fire station had a very large horn. This bull moose horn would have different blasts. Every household had a list of what they represented. Once and only once during my high school days did this sound ever occur. I don't remember how many blasts but it meant there was no school that day because it was so cold. I remember walking out on the back porch that morning, and I could not take a deep breath because it was very painful my lungs felt like they were collapsing. But as the day wore on and the weather warmed up, most of the children were out playing in the snow.

Trip to Fenway Park

The local priest was a huge baseball fan and he could take two boys to make a trip with him to Fenway Park to see a major-league baseball game. And I was one of those he picked. We had to leave early in the morning and stop in Keene, New Hampshire, to go to mass.

I had never been to mass before, and I remember getting up and down a lot, and the everlasting passing of the basket. It seemed like every time I looked up, the basket was in front of me looking for money.

We went on to Fenway Park and I saw some terrific baseball. I was just overwhelmed. I saw Ted Williams and Jimmy Piersall play, and I saw the famous Boudreau shift. It was a wonderful trip.

Barnum & Bailey Circus

My mother and Jimmy Wilmouth's mother decided it would be nice trip for my classmate Jimmy and me to go to the big circus at

Boston. So we headed out, the two moms and the two boys, and went to Barnum & Bailey Circus we saw things that you would never see unless you saw them in a book The many things I saw were so interesting an unusual that I can't describe them, except to say it was a great trip and we had a wonderful time.

Rodeo

The next year the moms decided it would be nice for us to go to the rodeo and I was pretty excited about this because I was into the Roy Rogers movies and all that stuff. I was more excited than Jimmy. It was very exciting, with lots of horses, Indians, cowboys, and all that stuff that I was interested in at that time. They had evening shows in the center of the arena which were terrific and we really enjoyed our first night there.

The next day we were having lunch at the famous Parker House. They were famous for their Parker House rolls, which are still around. While we were looking at the menu, the waiter asked us if we were down for the rodeo we said yes he said, "Well, I guess you came to see Roy Rogers," and we responded yes. He said, "Well I have a treat for you. If you look over there at that booth that's Roy Rogers."

I was so excited I could hardly stand it. He told us he would see if he could get his autograph. He came back and said yeah so we jumped out of the chairs and ran over. He signed a Parker House menu and said he hoped we enjoyed the show that night. And we surely did; this was a highlight of my young life and I never forgot it.

Jim sneezed the whole time we were there and didn't enjoy it is much as I did. Several weeks later we found out that Jim was allergic to horses.

My First Beer

Leading to the garage there was a large room Grandma used for storage. It was a place to accumulate a lot of empty bottles such as milk bottles and soft drink bottles, which were all refundable.

On one particular day she wanted to clean them out and take them to the little grocery store about three miles from the house. So I got the old Chrysler and backed it up to the garage door and we loaded up all of the old bottles that were refundable. We had quite a few, maybe twelve or thirteen. At the time, and I had learned to drive the Chrysler up at Lake Nineveh. So she let me drive down to Mr. Pitts' store.

I unloaded the bottles and took them into the store. She had a few items that she wanted to purchase. There were some Moxie bottles, which was a soft drink that was quite popular at this time, and several milk bottles. She told Mr. Pitts what she wanted and I loaded it in the Chrysler.

Just before we left she turned to me and said, "Would you like to have something?" and I said, "Yes, I want to six pack of Narragansett ale," which was a popular ale at that time. She told Mr. Pitts to get a six pack loaded into the truck and we went home with no comment from her whatsoever. That disappointed me because I thought she might raise cane with me but she didn't.

When we got home, we unloaded and put the stuff up, and she said, "You'd better put your beer in the refrigerator so it doesn't get hot." So I took it out of the back of the truck took it in the kitchen and put it in the refrigerator, lifting one bottle out. I sat down at the kitchen table, got an opener from the drawer. I took a couple of swigs, and it didn't taste very good so I just sat there and looked at her going about her business.

She never said a word to me and never discussed it. She paid absolutely no attention to me and did not make an issue of it, so I got up, put the bottle in the sink, and poured it out.

I guess Uncle John polished off the rest of the six pack. My grandmother never mentioned this incident ever. But I did find that she knew how to deal with me pretty good. If there was an issue, she knew how to deal with it without much commotion.

CHAPTER 2

School Days

The Leather Strap

My third grade teacher was Miss Keating, and she was a strict disciplinarian. She believed if you came to class you should learn something every day, and she made sure you had her full attention.

She kept a leather strap in her desk drawer. It was about six inches long, and about 1/4 of an inch thick, and if you needed discipline she would call you to the front, take out the leather strap hold your hand palm up, stretch it so the skin was tight. She would then administer a couple of severe whacks across the palm of your hand.

You could feel the sting and the others could see the blows. It only took one trip to the front to get you to pay attention in her class, which I am thankful for.

The Big Paddle

Unlike my third grade teacher Ms. Keating, I had a teacher later who had no control of her classroom. I do not remember her name. We would be throwing paper planes, rubber bands, and paperclips, and doing a lot of other disruptive stuff in her class most of the time. This particular classroom was located next to the stairwell that led to all the floors. The door to this classroom was partially covered with glass on top.

This particular day we were having a good time in her classroom raising hell. Our principal at this time was Mr. Calvin Lamont. It just so happened he peered into the glass window and raised his eyebrows at what he saw. He yanked the door open and stepped into the room and all became very quiet.

He called out about six boys' names and mine was included, and he stepped out in the hallway and told us to stand up against the wall and not to move till he came back. All of the students respected Mr. Lamont and feared him somewhat, and we did what we were told.

He returned shortly with his large paddle which he had received while at the University of Vermont. It had the team name Catamounts on it. It was shaped like a canoe paddle but smaller and very effective. He said, "Bend over and grab your ankles." We did.

I was a first in line next to the door in the hallway to receive my first whack. I was looking towards the stairwell and who should I spot but Grandma Davis. She was volunteering for the hot lunch program that day and was walking up the stairs. She stopped and observed and said nothing. He proceeded to paddle us good, three hard whacks apiece. Then he said, "Okay straighten up." He opened the classroom door and said, "Y'all can go back in and learn something today."

From that day on, that teacher's classroom was very orderly as we kept a close eye on the door most of the time. My grandmother never mentioned this incident, not that day or any day.

Walking to School

66 Main St. was located off Route 103 which is a short way from the high school. We used to walk to school every day. We'd have snowball fights in the wintertime and drink sap from the maple trees across the street from 66 Main St. The Sergeants had about ten maple trees out by the street and they would tap them when sugar season began. They would hang pails on the tree to catch the sap, and cover them so no trash would get into the sap. On the way to school, we could lift up the cover and take a sip of that sweet sap. If you drank too much you would surely get a good case of diarrhea so you had to be careful not to indulge too much.

It would be very cold and snowing some days in the wintertime, walking to school. Further uptown there was a concrete bridge over

Black River. And on these cold mornings some would put their mittens on the concrete bridge. They would be stuck until warmer weather came that day. So if you passed the bridge before noon, you would see a lot of mittens stuck on the bridge.

Sports

Before I was old enough to have a full-time summer job, I kept myself occupied playing with tennis balls, banging them up against the garage door. There were two large doors, and I could stand in the driveway with a tennis racket and whack away. I got the feel of hitting the tennis balls and it gave me some coordination with my feet, chasing them down and hitting them back. I loved to handle the tennis balls too and throw them against the garage door, and I developed a good feeling with my hands for the ball.

I seemed to be attracted towards the basketball too, and I had an old one that was pretty worn out. I had received a new one that Christmas that was rubberized so I could play outdoors in the wintertime with it. I got where I handled it all the time, even when I was in the bed at night. I would throw it up in the kitchen and I got to where I could dribble pretty good and enjoyed it very much.

I also had some baseballs, but no one to throw them to and play catch with. When I did find a partner, I learned to pitch on my own, and got very good at it while I was in junior high school. I was just a freshman in high school when I made the varsity baseball team and won several games that year. By the time I finished high school I had built a good reputation as a pitcher and had several big league scouts inquiring about me.

I didn't realize the significance of this at the time because I was only seventeen years old. Instead of entering college, I decided a year at a private college called Dean Academy in Franklin, Massachusetts, would be good for my development. So in the fall I enrolled at Dean Academy on a full scholarship.

Basketball and Baseball

These two sports were very big in my life growing up. I got good enough to play with some very talented athletes in both sports. When I was in high school I was scouted by several big-league scouts, but it just was not the right time for me to do any of that. I had a lot of living to do before jumping into such a profession as that.

During the summertime I played baseball with the American Legion team in Springfield, Vermont. We had some very talented players and had a top-notch coach, along with a very good team. We played all summer and won several games. We were picked to play in the playoffs in Claremont, New Hampshire.

Claremont had a young pitcher named Rudy Fortin. He was highly scouted, and he and I were selected to pitch the first game. It was a very tight game and we lost two to nothing but there were several scouts in the stands and they got a good look at both of us.

Rudy was a senior in high school, and he signed a contract with the Boston Red Sox. I never followed his career so I don't know what happened to him. I finished my senior year in high school and then went on to Dean Academy, which was a prep school.

Basketball trips

Some of our high school basketball trips were out of town and required a bus for transportation to the schools we were playing. The coaches, trainers, cheerleaders, and all the ballplayers rode the bus. The trips were in the wintertime, and the roads could be very dangerous due to snow and ice.

One such trip I remember very well was to Burr & and Burton Academy. The high school was located on the other side of the mountain called Big Bromley. The high school gymnasium was small and heated with steam heat. On each side of the gym were two large radiators covered with asbestos covers. When the referee handed you the ball out of bounds, you'd better not be up against one of those covers or you would get a hot seat.

We had very good drivers for our buses and never got into much trouble. This night however it had stormed really bad during the game. When we left, it was snowing really, really hard, and the roads were treacherous. We started up the mountain and got almost to the top when we got stuck. We had to stay there some time before help arrived to get us out back on the road.

You can imagine what a hard time the coaches had keeping the cheerleaders and the players separated. There was a lot of touchy-feely going on in the back of the bus but no harm was done. We arrived back in Ludlow sometime around two thirty in the morning. It was Saturday morning so nobody missed any school.

We had a trip to Poultney, Vermont, where we played their high school basketball team, and their gymnasium was also a place where they used to have school plays. There was a stage at one end covered with some heavy mats to keep players from hurting themselves if they got pushed into one of them.

About three quarters of the way through the ballgame, one of the players stole the ball from Jimmy Martin and was racing for a layup. Jimmy tried to block a shot and it ended up being a cross-body block. Jimmy and the other player skidded into the mats and all hell broke loose. The Poultney fans and our fans were out there with the players, and it was sometime before things calmed down. The game was postponed to a further date, and we had to be escorted out of town by the police. This was some scary night.

On our way back from Poultney we had to pass through Rutland, Vermont. There was a wonderful dairy bar called Seward Dairy Queen. They specialized in ice cream and made the best banana split you ever had. It was served in a trough-like dish. It had every kind ice cream you can imagine with plenty of bananas, chocolate syrup, marshmallows, whipped cream, and the cherry. There was no calorie counting that night, as we pigged out pretty good.

Trip to Boston with Coach Clairmont

Coach Clairmont had arranged a trip for the basketball team to go to Boston Garden. This is where the Boston Celtics and numerous other teams played. The hockey team also played there. They would cover the ice over with a parquet floor for the basketball teams to play on. I wondered what that would be like and later on in life I found out. When we stepped into the Boston Garden arena, one of my classmates, Winston Bixby said, Oh my dad could store a lot of hay in this place. We all just laughed.

While we were in Boston, we wanted to see as many sites as we could. We did see a lot of them. The one I remember most was a trip to the old Howard burlesque theater. This was supposed to be the oldest burlesque show in existence at the time. The coach went with us, and we watched the show in its entirety. This one lady dancer could twirl her pasties in opposite directions at the same time to the tune of *The Blue Danube* waltz.

Coach Clairmont was my typing teacher, and I sat in the back row. Once in a while I would lean back in my chair and make a gesture that he would recognize as the gesture used by the stripper. No one else could see me except Coach Clairmont, and he would smile a little bit and continue on with the class.

Visiting Boston Garden Again

When I was in prep school at the Academy I made a trip to the Garden and North Station Hotel. This was where all the athletes stayed when they played at Boston Garden. This particular trip I went to see a player named Bevo Francis. He was touted as the number one scorer in college basketball at the time. He had scored 113 points in one game. His team was traveling all over the country showing him off.

I went to the hotel and spotted Bevo sitting in a chair. He was very tall and was sprawled out pretty good. I took one look at his feet, and I had never seen such feet in my life. I found out his shoe size was seventeen and a half wide. I saw him play that night in the Garden and he could really shoot the basketball.

I later got to play on the parquet floor at Boston Garden when I played for the Bellows Falls Bears in a preliminary game against the Celtics. This was quite a treat for me and all the other players. Later on, I got to play against the famous Bob Cousy, who was my idol at the time. We played an exhibition game in Springfield, Vermont, and I guarded him for about five to ten minutes, and boy was that exciting. He was one terrific basketball player. I'll never forgot that day and still remember it well.

Stuck in the Snow

After a basketball game in high school, I had convinced this young lady to take a ride with me to the lake. It was pretty slow in the wintertime on all the roads up there, and there were some cottages that were vacated during the winter. They all had fairly long driveways leading up to them. This particular cottage had some large balsam trees on each side of the driveway. I could drive right up in there and the trees would hide the car from the road.

Well that's where we went we did a little smooching and so on. It was getting late and I knew she had to be home. I started to back the car out and got stuck in the snow. I was really panicked.

I was about half a mile from the nearest farm where my high school friend lived. His name was Donnie Ellison. His daddy had a big farm up there and that was my closest contact that night. I told her to sit tight and I would walk up to Ellison's. I did and of course it was late probably about 11:15 to 11:30. The lights were all out of the farmhouse, and I knocked on the back door.

Thank God Donnie came to the door and not his father. I told him what a predicament I was in, and he said, "Let me get the tractor and I'll put you out." He did pull me out and I took the girl home. I dropped her off at her house and I went on home to bed. This was in the middle of the week and on into the night, so I had to go to school the next day.

This doesn't sound like much of a story, but the little lady I was with was the principal's daughter. And I knew that when I went to school Wednesday, I was in for a big day. Around one o'clock that afternoon I was summoned to his office. He did all the talking, and I got to explain nothing. But he warned me not to be around his daughter again. I didn't need any further explanation, and I didn't date her. We were friends and stayed friends all through high school.

Other School Activities

Besides playing basketball and baseball, I was active in the band and played the second trumpet. I also was in the drama club and appeared in two or three plays. I really enjoyed playing my trumpet and could play by ear. I could hear a song and play it on my trumpet after hearing it a couple of times.

I still have my trumpet, and it's in very good shape. I'm unable to play it now, due to the fact that when I had chemotherapy and radiation I was advised to have all my teeth pulled. Without teeth to put pressure on the mouthpiece it's very difficult to get out a sound. I have a complete set of dentures uppers and lowers, but they don't seem to help very much. I still keep the trumpet and the valves oiled up and clean.

The Snowy Beer

My friend Johnny Paige worked at the local grocery store. We both thought it would be a good idea if we could get ahold of a six pack and hide it in the snow at the church after midnight mass. He got ahold of one, and that night it was pretty bad weather and snowing pretty hard. We buried the six pack in the snow and went to midnight mass.

The mass lasted a pretty good while and it was snowing pretty hard, and when we got out of church the snow had covered up our beer. We looked around for a little while, trying not to be suspicious. We couldn't find the beer. So we had to go home and the next morning we headed up there to see if we could find it. We had to wait till after dinner time for the snow to melt enough that we could see the top of the beer bottles. We gathered it up, and took it somewhere else for another day. We eventually disposed of it in a timely manner.

Square Dancing

In the summertime around the lakes and in the area where I lived, there were square dances every single night of the week almost. There were two favorite spots. One was at Benson's barn in Springfield, Vermont, and the other was at Lake Coolidge just outside of Ludlow, on Lake Rescue.

The Lake Coolidge one was where my uncle and all his friends went. They took their pickup trucks, backed them up to the side of the building, and lowered the sides where there would be plenty of fresh air all night. When I was young my uncle used to carry me along to sit on the truck and keep an eye on the beer. He would go by the icehouse prior to the dance, get a couple of big blocks of ice, and then put the beer in the back of the truck covered with a tarp. I would sit on the back of the truck, watching the square dance and wishing I was old enough to get in there and do some of that myself.

Finally one summer Uncle John just grabbed me and pulled me through the side of the building, and called to Ellen Parkhurst. She was the best dancer around at that time. He said, "Ellen, teach this boy how to dance." And boy did she teach me; she could do any kind of dance anyway and probably could've been a professional dancer. I learned from a very good teacher, and I have thanked her many, many times over the years because dancing got me into a lot of good places with a lot of nice ladies.

Driving the Truck in the Lake

I had a young lady in my class whom I had tried to date several times. She was going steady and would not go out with me. It was our senior year and upon graduation she was going to get married. I had convinced her that she should take a ride with me up by the lake. She said okay so I picked her up and we headed for Lake Rescue.

I had borrowed Uncle John's brand-new pickup truck to make the trip. Before we got to the lake, there was a place called Electric Lake Reservoir. It was close to the highway and fairly deep. The Chevrolet pickup I was driving had a knob underneath the glove compartment that said "warmer." I thought this was a good excuse for me to get a hold of her leg. So I reached over to turn the knob and at the same time feel her leg.

But when I reached over to do this, I pulled the steering wheel in the same direction. The next thing I knew, we were headed into the lake. The water was coming in, and I got her out, put her on the bank, and watched the truck sink a little deeper before it stopped.

A car came by and stopped and it was Jimmy Bresilin. He saw me and asked me what in the world happened. I told him and asked him to put the young lady in his car and take her back to Ludlow and tell Uncle John what had happened.

He did just that. In a little while, Uncle John showed up with a couple of his friends and took a look at the situation. The truck was not sinking any deeper, and the water was just up to the floorboards. One of his friends worked for the Benson Company, which had big wreckers. So they went back to town and got a large wrecker, attached it to the back end of the truck and started to winch it out of the water. It looked like it was going along pretty smoothly, but all of a sudden the truck twisted and rolled towards the lake.

They had to stop and take another look at what was going on. They decided to go get a jeep. They ran a cable through the cab to keep it from tipping towards the lake and as the winch pulled the truck backwards they kept the cable tight around the cab. There was not any damage to the truck, and the water did not get into the motor, which was lucky.

The young lady got home okay and got married two weeks later.

Several years later when I was visiting Vermont, I went by to visit her at her father's store, and we laughed about that incident that day.

WWL New Orleans

We used to hang out at the ice cream parlor, sometimes sitting on the front steps and listening to music. I used to tune into WWL New Orleans and listen to their great jazz. I often wondered what it was like in New Orleans and hoped I would get to go there one day and hear this great music live. Later on in this memoir, I will tell about my various trips to New Orleans when I got older. And it did not disappoint me. New Orleans is a great place with great entertainment and terrific music.

Class of 1953 Senior Class Trip

Oh boy, our class trip was coming up. We all wanted to go to New York City, and we had raised enough money to make this trip. There were chaperones assigned to us, and Mr. Bullis, who was a principal of the high school, was one of them. We were all staying in the same hotel, the boys on one floor, the girls on the next floor. Mr. Bullis had his hands full keeping us separated, but he managed pretty well, and we got to see some great shows. I saw the Rockettes, which was a famous dance group at Radio City Music Hall, and they were wonderful. There's so many things I could say about this trip but I don't believe I could do it justice, other than saying we had a great time and nobody got into any trouble.

The Bryant Family

The Bryant family was from Florida and they came to Vermont in the summertime. They were a wealthy family with a grandmother who was known as B.B. Bryant and who was a majority stockholder in the manufacturing plant in Springfield, Vermont, called Bryant Chuck and Grinder. She stayed in Springfield most of the time and her children lived in Florida.

The family had a big piece of property on Lake Rescue with several nice buildings. There was a bunkhouse, a main house, and a big summerhouse with a large patio for entertaining. There were two children around my age: Cynthia, who was a little bit older maybe a year, and Billy, who was maybe a year younger than me.

I dated Cynthia a few times and became very friendly with the whole family. Billy used to like to hang around with me and always wanted to go over to New York State. In the state of Vermont at that time, you had to be twenty-one years old to purchase alcohol. In New York State the legal limit to purchase alcohol was eighteen. And there was a club in New York State just over the line, called Hampton Manor. They used to have big-name bands, and big-name entertainers. They had great music, and you could buy a drink if you could put your chin on the bar. So that was a quite a good place to go and have a good time for the young folks.

Billy kept after me to take him there, and I finally agreed. His dad had given him a brand-new automobile, a Hudson Hornet. It was fast and really sporty looking. So one evening I told him I would take him over there and he could follow me in his car. My Uncle John had a new Chevrolet and it was in the driveway. I knew where the keys were and he was not around. So I borrowed the car for the night, and called Billy and told him to meet me at the Red Bridge. It was kind of foggy that night, and I told him to follow me and I would lead him out to the main highway and there he could keep up with me good.

The back roads around the lake were all dirt, and the branch in the road was just beyond the bridge. I had taken a right turn, and I had gone a little way and I did not see his headlights. So I waited a few minutes, and he didn't show up so I started backing up slowly. It was really foggy and I couldn't see very well, so I was careful, but not careful enough. I banged right into the front of the Hudson Hornet and mashed the rear end of the bumper on John's Chevrolet pretty bad. There was no damage to the car mechanically, and off we went to Hampton Manor.

We had a great time, and it was about four o'clock in the morning when we got back. I drove the Chevy into the driveway, hung up the keys, and went to sleep on the back porch. I knew that when Uncle John woke up and took one look at that Chevrolet he would be highly perturbed. Well he was pretty upset and he woke me up and said, "What the hell did you do with my car last night?"

I told him what had happened, and he said it was okay since it could be fixed. I sure gave him a lot of grief with his vehicles while I was a youngster. He never got really mad with me and was always very good to me.

Trip to New York City with Hank Meeker

Hank was my cousin from British Columbia and his mother Bessie Meeker was my grandmother's sister. He had come to Vermont one summer to stay a few weeks, and we decided to take a trip to New York City. He had a sister named Joy who was a star in a radio soap opera called *Amanda of Honeymoon Hill*.

Joy was married to a famous songwriter named Charles Kenny. His company was named Goldmine in the Sky. It was named after a song he had written for Gene Autry in this movie called *Goldmine in Sky*. He also had written and published a couple of other big name songs such as *Gone Fishing* and *Love Letters in the Sand*, which Pat Boone made famous.

Hank and I had the best time and on the way there we spent the night in Connecticut in a summer place that Joy and Mr. Kenny had. That was where I saw my first television program. It was a professional wrestling show on a very small screen.

When we got to New York City, they showed us all over the place. They lived in a penthouse somewhere near United Nations building. One night they took us out to a place where I had my first grilled pork chop. We had a great time and headed back to Ludlow.

Hank Meeker went on to become a prominent doctor in Minneapolis, Minnesota. I talked to him a few years ago he was still practicing.

Jimmy Bresilin's Dance Bar

Jimmy Bresilin was a Realtor, and had several cottages located on Lake Rescue. These cottages were rented mostly by executives from the city. They would bring their families for a whole summer. Most of them had daughters who were around my age. Jimmy had a barn for dancing. About two nights a week he would have a dance at the barn.

I don't know how I got in with this crowd, but boy I did have a good time. I developed a real crush on a young lady named Barbara Crippen, who was from Tenafly, New Jersey. She was a year older than I and headed off to college when she returned home from the vacation. She knitted me a pair of argyle socks. And in the toe of each sock was her nickname, Boots. I kept the socks a long time. She went on to college at Duke University and I finished my senior year at Black River High School.

The Big Yellow Dump Truck

During the summertime I used to drive this truck for my uncle. He always had a job for me and I enjoyed it. He would contract the truck out for the job and I would drive it all week long. When the day was done, we used to drive the truck to a parking place where all the vehicles were stored at night. In the morning when we left for the work, we would get in our vehicles and drive to the location.

This particular morning it was kind of foggy, and I had started up the truck and let it warm up a little bit. I started to back up and felt the truck was in kind of a rut. I rocked it back and forth a little bit and it seemed to be okay. I then gave it plenty gas, backed up, and somebody shouted, "Whoa whoa, Babe!" I stopped the truck and got out.

The rut I was in was the hood of somebody else's car. I had crushed it in pretty good. John came over and said, "Oh my God, what else did you get into?" I went on to work and I guess the insurance paid for the man's car. John never did fuss at me. When we did have a contract for the truck, the truck stayed at 66 Main St. in the driveway.

I had a date with a young lady from Springfield, Vermont, to go to the drive-in one night. I had dated her several times, and she was a really nice girl. I found myself without a vehicle to take her to the drive-in. The only thing available was the big yellow dump truck. I took off for Springfield and pulled up in front of her house. Her father was sitting on the porch. He took one look at that truck and said, "Where are you going with that thing?" I told him to the drive-in, and he said okay, and we headed to the drive-in theater.

The speaker wire was not long enough to hang on the window, so I had to place it on the floorboard. I'm sure everybody looked at us and wondered what in the hell we were doing. We had a great time and watched a good show and I took her home that night I headed back to Ludlow. Mission accomplished.

Woody the Nurse

My uncle John had got engaged to a nurse named Woody, and she stayed at 66 Main St. while he was overseas. While she was staying with us, I developed pneumonia one winter. She really took care of me and I don't know what I would have done without her.

She had a car, and I had a driver's license. I kept after her to let me borrow the car to go to Windsor, Vermont. She said, "What you want to go there for?" I told her I wanted to see my father, and she said, "Well I'll just drive you over there." I finally had to explain to her that he was in the federal penitentiary at Windsor, Vermont. She then let me borrow the car to go.

I was pretty excited and also very nervous about this. You can imagine a sixteen-year-old boy who had seen his father only a few times, going to the state penitentiary to visit him. I went, and it was quite an experience to say the least. Steel doors, the bars, all of that made me very nervous. I went into this big room where there was a big long table.

I sat down and in a few moments my father came into the room, sat across from me, and the conversation was very awkward. He acted like nothing was wrong, but everything was wrong. I was disappointed that he was so nonchalant about the whole situation. I drove back home and tried to forget the trip.

I saw my father two more times in his lifetime. The next time was after I graduated from high school during the summer. My grandmother told me not to go live with him because he was trouble. Well I went anyway, and she was right. At that time he was head chef at the Berwick Hotel in Rutland, Vermont. He made me his second cook, which was a joke. I peeled potatoes and washed dishes all summer. That was the downside. The upside was I got to eat all the scallops and best food the hotel offered. I found out then that he was an alcoholic.

I left, and shortly thereafter I joined the service. I saw him one more time when I took my future wife Sylvia to Vermont to visit my family. On the way back I found out he was living in Connecticut and made arrangements to see him so he could meet Sylvia.

He was living in this big house out in the country with two new dogs that were bad. I didn't know what he was doing and really didn't care. We stayed there just long enough to eat out and move on. This is the last time I ever saw my father.

After I was married and had children he wrote me a letter telling me how proud he was of me and a lot of other b.s. The letter so infuriated me that I wrote him a nasty letter and told him that he had no right to call me SON. I told him he had never done anything but bring shame to the Barnard name. And I never wanted to hear from him again. And I never did. His sister notified me of his death. Case closed.

My New Model A Roadster

I had purchased this Model A Roadster from Helen Murphy for 100 bucks. It had been sitting in her garage for some time and needed a lot of work. We had to tow it to the house, and I was really excited about fixing it up. Grandfather had built me some new stays for the canvas convertible top. I found the person to make me a custom convertible top.

I had gone to the Catholic church when they were remodeling the altar, and got several pieces of the bright red rug that were never used. I used them to cover the two side panels and the rumble seat. I spray-painted the wheels silver. This was a sporty model and I had a lot of fun in it. It had a manifold heater, and was not conducive to drive in the wintertime. So I parked it in the garage most of the winter. I used to drive it at dinner time up to the ice cream parlor with a load of kids during lunchtime. We would have a sandwich and a milkshake and head back to school.

On the way back to school one day I heard this kind of a clunking sound on the ground. Four times. The rear wheel came off and went flying past me, headed for the fire station garage door. It hit the door and broke a few of the glass panes and then stopped. I didn't know what caused this until I looked up in the road and saw the lug nuts lying in the road. I backtracked and picked them all up — there weren't many — and retrieved the wheel and walked back to the car. A couple of boys were walking by and just lifted up the rear end and I put the wheel back on. Nobody was hurt, but it could've been very dangerous.

There was a young lady my high school a year ahead of me, who was a cheerleader. We all used to hang out at the ice cream parlor and visit. I had always wanted to take her out, but she had an older boyfriend who watched her like a hawk. She lived behind the ice cream parlor in a big house facing the other side of the street. I devised a plan to take her to the lake. I had talked about it several times with her and she seemed interested.

I finally put the plan in operation and drove my Model A around the back of the ice cream parlor. I told her to go get in the front seat and cover up with a blanket. She went out the back door and got in the car and covered up. I looked around and knew she had gone to the car, so I just went around the side started the old Model A and drove out the driveway onto the street. Her family had a beautiful cottage on the lake, and we had a good afternoon of swimming. I brought her back the same way, took her to her house, and no one knew the difference. I knew that she never told and neither did I. It was great fun.

CHAPTER 3

Lake Ninevah

Building the Cabin

My grandparents started building a cabin in 1946. I was eleven years old at the time and I don't know why the spot for the cabin was picked out. The only thing I know about that is that it was part of a large (1,000 acres) piece of land around Lake Ninevah owned by my grandmother's father, Moses Townsend, and the last piece of property, around 360 acres, was sold some fifteen years later on October 14, 1960.

Kelly Foster and Sawyer Hill bought it for $8,000. The documents were submitted to the court on October 21, 1960 by Alan Fletcher Junior. Alan died on November 11, 1960 at Springfield Hospital according to his wife.

My grandmother kept a daily journal while the cabin was being built, and all the activities that went on around it for the next fifteen years. It was a detailed account of all the activities and the people who were involved and everyone who enjoyed the wilderness surrounding the cabin. I will not try to duplicate any of her dictation and I will list only the incidents that I recall, that I was personally involved with.

Grandma, Grandpa, and I used to go to Lake Ninevah daily while we were building the cabin. Grandpa and I would drive the old Chrysler to the farmhouse on the property where Grandma had been born years ago, and we would salvage what lumber we could get. I would take the nails out of the boards and we loaded them into the old Chrysler truck and drove to the cabin.

Uncle John and all his friends worked very hard to get to cabin started. When it was livable, Grandma, Grandpa, and I stayed up there all the time, and Grandpa and I worked very hard trying to complete the cabin.

Grandpa's Accident

On June 11, 1947, Grandpa Davis had a bad accident. He was coming home from work, sitting on the tailgate of a dump truck with his friend Alan Merrill, who was also a carpenter. He was holding some kind of a window frame, and coming down from Buttermilk Falls. A car coming from the other way collided with the truck. Grandpa tumbled over a couple of times and hit his head on the truck body and broke his neck.

They rushed him to the Rutland Hospital. Leon came to the cabin and got Grandma and me and drove us to Tyson, where the Chases were meeting Grandma. They drove us on to the hospital where Grandpa was. He was in a room by himself in traction with a collar around his neck and unconscious. The doctors told my grandmother that his condition was very serious.

It was a stormy night with a lot of thunder and lightning. I sat in the chair in the back of the room, and Grandma sat by his bedside. Sometime in the middle of the night, I heard my grandpa mumble a sound, and he said, "Dolly, Dolly, don't leave me." Grandma responded, "I'm right here, Clarence, I'm not going to leave you."

Grandpa was a big man, over six foot three and around 225 pounds. I had never seen him as I saw him that night in the bed; it was a real shock.

Grandpa did survive and stayed in the hospital for a couple of months. We brought him home to 66 Main St. but that halted any cabin activity for the rest of the year. He stayed in the front bedroom in the bed most of the time, as he was not able physically to support himself.

I sat by his bedside nearly every day when I got home from

school. And we did a lot of visiting. Grandpa used to squeeze tennis balls all the time, little by little getting his strength back.

Several Sundays had passed and we were all eating dinner in the kitchen. We heard a thumping sound, coming from the area of the bedroom, and wondered what the world it was. In a few minutes Grandpa came walking in with his cane, and said, "I'm kind of hungry."

From that day on he never went back in the bed except sleep at night. He was the very tough guy. That winter and spring Grandpa became as active as he could. When the weather warmed up, Grandpa, Grandma, and I headed for Lake Nineveh and stayed all summer long.

The Stone

This stone is a landmark that is still in place today. This is how it got there.

Grandpa had courted Grandma when she was young and living in Ninevah. She had grown up on a farm about two miles from where we later built the cabin. Her family originally owned 1,000 acres, which they sold off in parcels over time, keeping only one parcel for themselves. That last parcel was very important to Grandma, and that's where we built the cabin.

Grandpa had visited the property several times in his youth and was familiar with the old house and barns. He remembered a beautiful slab of polished marble in front of the house.

He told me, "Babe, we're going to get that big marble stone and put it by the front door at the cabin and dedicate it to Maggie." I said okay not knowing what we were in for.

The old Chrysler car had been cut down to a truck. It was just planks across the back with no sideboards. I had learned to drive it up at the lake. So Grandpa and I loaded up the old Chrysler and headed for the old house and the barn area. Grandpa knew about where to look and he told me to go get the pry bar and a couple of shovels and head over to the barn.

*Clarence and Maggie Davis
at Lake Ninevah, 1951.*

He walked over to the old house, which had fallen in pretty bad, and he said, "Start digging right around in here." I dug around for a little while and it was grown over pretty bad, and he said, "Now poke around and see if you can hit something solid in the ground. I did and sure enough *clank clank clank*. Grandpa was excited and said, "That's where the stone is." So I proceeded to dig all around until I got all the dirt and grass off the top.

There was this huge marble slab a little bit bigger than a card table, solid black, with white streaks all through it. It was really quite pretty. So I cleaned off all way around it got it where we could get a good look. He said, "Now we're going to get it on the truck and take it to the cabin."

I couldn't believe he thought we could load that whole big thing on the truck with him in a chair and me only twelve years old, but that never entered his mind. So we went back to camp that day. The next morning, we loaded the truck with the pry bar, block and tackle rope, and shovels. And we headed back over to do our chore. He also had me load two house rollers which were about five and a half to six feet long that he had used in his work as a carpenter.

Grandpa sat in this wooden chair, and I unloaded the supplies. "The first thing to do, Babe, is to back the truck up close to the slab and put the brakes on and dig all around the front of the slab until you get the pry bar under there pretty good."

I did all that, and then waited for further instructions. He said, "Now get that stone over there to get some leverage under the pry bar and try to remove the stone off its setting," and I did. I moved the pry bar and leveraged the block all around the front so I got it pretty loose. He then said, "Get a little more leverage and raise it up as high as you can, and I'll slide this roller underneath the front," and he did that. We had made some kind of progress at this point.

Now we had to hook the block and tackle to the stone and around a tree that was close by so we could do some pulling. The stone had some very rough edges where it had been cut from the quarry and never finished. So the rope was easily tied. I did all that and handed him the rope, and we began to pull the rope through the pulley. Little by little we raised up the slab and moved the roller farther towards the middle of the stone.

He told me to get back in the truck and back it up flush with the stone as we had it partially standing on end. I did. We then secured the stone with the rope in that position. He had me tie another rope around the front of the stone at a different angle with another pulley to move the stone forward. He then told me to get in the truck and back it up again flush against the stone and I did. The stone was secured upright and we pulled the rope forward and the stone tipped towards the truck. The truck brakes were on so the truck would not move when the stone was tipped forward.

He then had me place a roller on the flatbed truck and block it so could not move backwards. Then we lowered the stone and tipped it forward onto the roller. We then were able to release the block and tackle that was holding the stone upright and he had me go secure the very back of the stone with the rope through the pulley.

With the stone on the roller, it was time to place the other roller towards the front of the stone so it would roll completely on the truck and as we pulled the block and tackle forward, the stone moved very easily onto the truck bed.

I never would've believed that we would get that big stone on the truck ready to take to the cabin. With the right tools and knowledge, Grandpa could move just about anything. I learned all about leverage and fulcrum. The biggest thing I learned was being prepared, having a plan and being patient to execute the plan. I was only twelve at that time but that taught me a very good lesson.

We proceeded to take the stone to the cabin and were done for the day. The next day it was easy to unload and we had already had a place to put the stone leveled out so it would sit flat. That stone was placed there in 1947 and is still there to this day. I have pictures of it which I took last week on July 21, 2019.

I was able to take my three grandchildren along with my wife up to Vermont for a vacation around twenty years ago. I wanted to visit the cabin and see if the stone was still there. I had rented a car and drove up to Lake Nineveh, and up to the cabin. It had been remodeled and looked really good and the stone was still there. I stepped on the stone and stomped my feet and really teared up.

The Bass That Got Away

Grandpa Davis had built me a nice flat-bottom boat which I painted gray. It had the oarlocks and everything. I used to go out in that boat nearly every day and try to catch those big old bass. There were hardly any people around the lake at that time so it was very peaceful and very quiet. By the dam was a large rock where I used to anchor the boat and look in the water and see those huge bass swimming around.

I had tried every single bait I had in my tackle box and could not produce results. So I decided this day I would grapple them and try to snatch them out of the water. I don't how long I'd been staring in the water looking at the fish but the next thing I remember, Grandma was throwing cold water on me trying to get me to wake up. I evidently had passed out in the boat, which was close to the rock so she could tiptoe on the other rocks out to the big rock and rescue me, and she did so many times. I went back to camp and rested the rest of the day and I never was able to catch one of those big bass.

The Island

There was an island some distance from the shore towards the other side of the lake. I used to row the boat over there and check out the island. There was a lot of wildlife coming and going on the island as the tracks revealed. My main goal was to be able to swim to the island and back before the end of the summer. Grandma would get in the boat and row alongside me and I would start to the island. I made several attempts and finally before the summer ended I was able to accomplish my goal. And it made me feel pretty good that I had accomplished this.

My grandmother and grandfather had taught me how to swim, while sitting on the dock with me in the water. The beach was purely sand and you could walk out for about 100 yards in sand. My grandmother surely loved this place, as you will see in my later recollections.

Seeing the Moon

One day Grandma, Grandpa, and I were down at the dock, and they were continuing to teach me how to swim. Grandma was sitting on the dock with her feet in the water, and Grandpa was in the water with me. We were in almost waist-high water, and Grandpa had on one of those old-time bathing suits. Since his accident he was slumped over on his right side somewhat, and the strap would sometimes fall off the shoulders.

This particular day he turned to Grandma and said, "Did you ever see the moon come up?" She said no and I had no idea what he was talking about. He pulled the straps on his bathing suit all down and he went underwater. He turned a somersault I guess underwater and his big behind was sticking straight up in the air. He stood up, pulled his bathing suit straps up, and said to her, "Did you see the moon come up?' Her comment was, "I did and it was a full moon." How we laughed about that. We had such a good time.

The Airplane
When we were at the cabin some days in the afternoon, we would hear an airplane nearby. The plane would fly so low overhead it would scrape the tops of some of the trees and make a heck of a noise. The plane would then go out over the lake and roll from side to side dipping its wings almost in the water. This was quite dangerous, but this pilot was a dangerous guy. His name was Arnold Lawson. He had been a pilot in the service and would go to Rutland airport to rent a plane. He would do this several times. I think he enjoyed it very much.

Clambakes
We used to have several clambakes during the summer at the cabin. John and his friends would buy several bags of clams and bring them to the cabin on Friday night. They would pour them into big washtubs, of which we would have about three. Then they would pour cornmeal all over the tops of the clams in the tub. The cornmeal would sit in the tubs all night with the clams, and evidently this was a cleaning process that the clams would use cleanse their digestive system.

There would be a least half a dozen big garbage cans with burners and baskets attached to them. The clams would be placed in the baskets and steamed over boiling water. The side dish was plenty of melted butter with lots of saltine crackers, and plenty of beer. This was fine eating, and a lot of people would show up for our clam-bakes. They would pitch horseshoes, swim in the lake, and some would play badminton. The clambakes would last all day, and people would head to the square dance at Lake Coolidge on Saturday night.

The Hotdog

John and his friends managed to get ahold of a large pontoon raft. This raft was used to transport heavy motor vehicles and tanks across water during the war. In the middle of this gigantic raft was a large inflatable tube that looked like a giant hotdog. It took nearly a whole day to put air in this gigantic raft. We anchored it to the end of the dock, and boy did we have a lot of fun playing on it. For a long time they had a big air compressor that put the air in. This large raft would hold twenty or twenty-five people at one time. Take the hotdog out, try to stand on top of it was almost impossible. It surely was a great addition to the lakefront.

The Real Dog Red

My stepdad Pat loved the outdoors; he loved to track and hunt coon. One summer he had brought me a puppy, which was a red bone hound we named Red. He wanted me to keep it for the summer so he could hunt with it in the fall. This puppy became my companion and closest friend. All summer we played together, roamed the woods and swam in the lake. He was very smart and easy to train and I did some of this every day.

I remember one day showing off to my grandfather. I told him I could put a piece of meat over the dog's nose and tell him, "No, Red." I said he would just do as I had told him to do. Grandpa said he would never do that, and I proceeded to show him that he would, and he did.

He grew very strong and big. He had a dog house on top of the hill but he never stayed up there because he slept by my bed at night. Summer was coming to a close, and it would soon be time to take the dog hunting. When that day came, I wanted to show off how good the dog would mind. So I sent him to the doghouse on top of the hill and told him to stay.

Pat said, "Where's the dog?"

"On top of the hill," I said.

Pat called him, but the dog did not come. He called again and again.

I said, "He won't come until I call him."

He was surprised and said, "Okay, call him."

I did so, and the dog came and Pat was impressed.

Well we headed out coon hunting that night and it wasn't long before we struck a trail. There are two kinds of hunting dogs, open trailers and silent trailers. All of Pat's dogs were open trailers, and soon they were all barking. In a little while, the sound changed. When we got to the dog, Red was covered in porcupine quills. I had never seen so many quills in my life, and he was in terrible pain. Pat told one of the Pratt boys, "Take Babe, get the truck and get some pliers." So we headed back towards the truck. I heard a gunshot. I didn't know what that was, but I soon found out. Pat had shot Red.

I was so hurt I cried and cried. It was several weeks before I would even speak to Pat. I soon realized that that was the only choice he had. The summer ended on a sour note for me. School would soon be starting and I would have to move on.

Prince Albert Tobacco Can

It was a rainy day at cabin and we were all inside. Somebody got out the fiddle and started playing. Well we are all soon clapping and having a gay time. Leon was really dancing. He jumped up on the bed, and was jumping down when his ankle hit the iron rod and he cut his ankle really bad. He was bleeding pretty bad, and Grandpa got the Prince Albert can, which was full of balsam blisters. He proceeded to clean the wound, cut open several blisters, and apply their resin to the wound. He covered the wound and bandaged it good.

That stopped the activity for the day and Leon had to lie down with his foot elevated the rest of the day. He went to the doctor in town the next day, and the doctor said it was okay, gave him a shot and bandaged it up again. It healed up very fast. Sometime later Leon was dancing again, and the matches in his pocket caught on fire. Boy did he come out of his pants and hurry to get some water. No damage but a lot of excitement.

Pat's Traps

Pat was an excellent trapper; he was meticulous about preparation for setting his traps. He would boil all of the traps in a large washtub, with some hemlock branches. He would then coat them with some kind of bluish substance and hang them out to dry. He would never touch them again. He had a large hook, and all the traps had a ring at the end where he could pick them up and hang them up to dry. He wore the same clothes and gloves when setting up his traps. He kept a small bottle with an eyedropper which he could use to drop scent on the traps. He used them to catch foxes and other animals.

He would set the trap line early in the morning, about two dozen traps. There are two sets of traps; one is called a wet set and the other is a dry set. The dry set was set out away from water, and the wet set was set along the creek bank. He used crab apples as bait for muskrat, mink, and beaver. He would run his trap lines in the evening when he got off work.

He would then take the catch of the day back to the shop where he would skin everything he had caught. He would then put the skins on a stretch board. These boards were V-shaped, probably about eighteen to twenty inches long, and very sturdy. He would strap them to the board and scrape the fat off. He would do this every day, and after two or three weeks he would have quite a cache.

The man who bought furs would come by. They would barter for the price of all of the furs. This was quite an interesting thing to watch, as Pat was very good at this. Most of the time the deal was settled with cash, but sometimes the trader would go to his vehicle and come back with a gun of some kind. He would offer this to Pat to boot. This would clinch the deal.

CHAPTER 4

Summer Jobs

Dump Truck Driver

My uncle John always got me a job on construction in the summertime. He had a big yellow dump truck, and I used to drive it all summer. Five days a week he would contract his truck for a job and I would drive it to the job every day. It was an easy job but was some responsibility. All the guys I hung around with used to swim at Red Bridge. It was pretty deep and cold and we would dive into it from the top of the bridge. Most of us had a cake of soap that we kept under the bridge in a plastic case.

After work every day, I would drive the yellow truck down to the bridge, pull off to the side, and strip down to my skivvies. I would then climb up on the bridge and dive into the water. It was cold and refreshing. I would swim underneath the bridge, get my bar soap, climb back up on top of the bridge, soap up good, dive back in the water maybe once or twice, and that was my bath for the day. I would then go home for supper and get dressed.

There was a square dance somewhere close by five days a week and I used to try to hit every one of them.

Camp Counselor

When I was sixteen, I took I took a summer job at the YMCA camp at Lake Fairly. It was a coed team and it had a beautiful lake that separated the boys on one side and the girls on the other. We all ate and had our meetings in the big center lodge. I was assigned about eight boys, and they were all from the city and had never been to anyplace like this. We all had a great time and learned some crafts and sat around the campfire at night telling spooky stories.

One of the favorite activities was to take the canoes out and paddle up into a marshy area. There were plenty of small turtles about the size of a paper plate, and we would take a canoe paddle, scoop them up into the canoe, and paint their yellow bellies with our name and the date in red nail polish. We would then put them back in the water. Some of the children would come back the following year and catch the turtles, and some of them would have the same painting on them. It was a grand summer and I really enjoyed it.

The Hardware Store

I also had worked at the local hardware store in Ludlow, Vermont, which was owned by Mr. Devereaux. He had a son named Donnie, who was my age and he also worked there part time. Donnie had convinced his dad that it would be a nice trip to go to Montréal and come down the New York side to Vermont. He finally convinced him.

His dad had a new Chevy automobile and we loaded up and headed for Montréal. We spent a couple of nights and days in Montréal seeing the sights and purchasing about four or five pints of Dark Horse Ale. We hid it under the back seat and went on our way. We came down the New York side and saw Santa's workshop, Lake Placid where all the rich folks stayed, and the North Pole which had a lot of Christmas decorations and scenery. We then came down the Vermont side and drove back to Ludlow. Boy did we have a good time.

The Funeral Home

I also worked for Jack Spalding, who lived across the street from us as he was married to one of the Sargent daughters. He owned the local funeral home and would go and pick up bodies to carry to the funeral home. Since I lived across the street, he could get ahold of me most anytime to help out. He paid me very well and I had several trips during the summer with him.

The first body I ever picked up was a young female who was pregnant around age twenty-five, and had passed way in the doctor's office. It was in Wallingford, Vermont, which was about forty minutes from where we were. We drove over there and entered the doctor's office and her body was lying on the table in the back. We had a gurney and a body bag, which we loaded her into. Mr. Spalding told me to get the legs and he would take the front. We picked her up and placed her in the body bag and zipped it up. For a long time I had this clammy feeling from handling that body. I got over it and did several more jobs for him.

My Pulpwood Job

I also had a job that lasted only about two weeks. I was hired to drive a pulpwood truck to Mechanicsville, New York, to the paper mill. I was told I would have some money to pay someone to load the truck for me, and my job was to drive it to the paper mill and return it to be loaded the next day. It sounded pretty good to me and the pay was very good. So I took the job.

On the first day, the truck was loaded, and I drove her to Mechanicsville, helped unload it into the big water tank, and drove truck back. I had to leave early in the morning, and the next morning when I drove down to take the truck to the paper mill it was empty. No one had loaded it, so that was left up to me. This was hard work and took a long time but I did load it and drove it to the paper mill and returned it.

I thought there had been some kind of miscommunication and let it slide. The next morning the truck was empty, and I had to load it again. I did this for the week and confronted my boss Friday afternoon. He paid me and said he was sorry that there would be somebody there Monday. Well it never happened, I loaded the truck three more times, and on Thursday morning I left him a note on the truck that I quit. I saw him that Friday, and he paid me for the three trips. I'd made extra for having to load the truck. He apologized, and I moved on to something else.

— PART 2 —
U.S. ARMY YEARS

CHAPTER 5

Enlistment and Training

Decisions

In October 1955 my friend Johnny Paige and I enlisted in the U.S. Army. We had enlisted for an additional period of two years, and we arrived at the induction center somewhere in New Hampshire I think it was Claremont. Somewhere between the time we left Vermont and got to Claremont, New Hampshire, Johnny decided it would be a good idea if we became ballistic meteorologists. I had no idea what he was talking about but he said the pay was a lot better and the benefits would be better if we were in this category. So when we got there we told the induction sergeant that that's what we wanted to do, he said that would be fine.

The hitch was we had to extend for one more year in order to go to ballistic meteorologist school, and we had to be warrant officers. In order to be a warrant officer you had to have at least thirty-six months of active duty. So we did, which was a big mistake.

We were sent to Fort Dix, New Jersey, to do our basic eight-week training. And it was horrible. I guess it's the way it's supposed to be to make you a better soldier. The language I heard was unreal. A big old tall, lanky sergeant from Texas greeted us on the bus. He said we were assigned to the company named Dog Company, and we'd be treated just like dogs. It wasn't quite that bad, but it was something I was not used to — or any of us probably.

I had my first Army buddy when we got to camp. The housing was very modern and new and clean. My buddy was an ex-Marine who had enlisted back into the U.S. Army. He was well trained and

The author at Fort Benning, Georgia, 1956.

knew a lot of shortcuts and kept us out of trouble most of the time. In the course of our training during the eight weeks we had to go out and bivouac for one week in the field. We had to pitch a tent, lay out all our stuff for inspection and sleep in the tent every night and fall out for *Reveille*.

It was pretty cold at Fort Dix in the latter part of October and November. Boyd was my friend's best name, and he told me before we went to bivouac, to go buy several candles at the PX. I didn't know what for but I trusted him and him did so. When we got to the campsite we pitched our tents and got up for inspection. Every soldier had been issued the same equipment, which included a steel pot helmet. This helmet would fit well with your regular helmet and was very heavy and made of steel. We were settled in and getting ready to crawl into our tents for the night.

Boyd had gotten about four of the steel pots and had them inside our little tent. He put one in every corner of the tent. He then took his bayonet and made a deep cross trench in the same location. He put the candles in the ground deep enough to make them secure and packed dirt around them, and lit the candles and placed the steel pots on top of them. The deep small trenches underneath the pots allowed oxygen for the candles to burn.

Soon the pots began to be red hot and put out a lot of heat. I can remember lying there in our shorts and T-shirts while these pots were putting out heat. I'm sure the others, in other tents were freezing their butts off. It took about three hours for the candles to burn down and the temperature to drop. But every night we had a nice warm tent for a short period of time, thanks to Boyd.

I also became good friends with a boy named George Fellows, who was from Syracuse, New York, and we hit it off pretty good. His friendship turned out to be valuable to me during my whole time in the service. I will not waste my time going into basic training, only to say I was glad to leave.

Johnny Paige and I finished basic training and were headed back to Vermont for Christmas. We met a young man from Weston, Vermont, who had a Volkswagen and he was going back to his home also. We hitched a ride and started back. It was really snowing and pretty bad weather and we had to drive slow. Once we got off the turnpike and out in the countryside, we spotted a nice-looking place with several cars in the parking lot. We knew this must be a good place to eat so we pulled in and had our first meal away from the military. We had a couple glasses of wine and a fine meal and loaded up and headed to Ludlow. I never was so glad to be home in my whole life.

New Assignment
Johnny Paige and I were both assigned to go to Camp Chaffee, Arkansas, for artillery training. We had a few days before we were

to report after Christmas and enjoyed our stay at home. One of my high school classmates Arden Peplaw was home on leave, and was assigned to report to Fort Benning, Georgia, so we hitched a ride with him. The reason we went to Fort Benning was that Johnny Paige's brother-in-law was a full bird colonel and stationed at Fort Benning. This was the first time the three of us had ever been south and we saw some wonderful territory and ate some good food and saw some pretty women. We arrived at Fort Benning and Arden had a go to his company and Johnny stayed with his brother-in-law. We drank a few beers and spent a couple of days there, and had to take a train to Fort Chafee. We had about a three-hour layover in Birmingham, Alabama, so we got off the train and decided to look around town. It was a big city, one we had never seen and wanted to explore what we could in the short time we were there.

We wandered into town and came upon the movie theater. The movie was just letting out and the people were coming out of the theater. I believe I saw the most gorgeous women I have ever seen in my life. I told Johnny Paige when I got through with the service business this was where I was going to settle down. He just laughed at me.

We went on to Chaffee, which was an artillery training post, and we learned to be fire direction control operators. The weather was nasty; it was raining and cold. On the weekends I found where they were playing basketball on the post and got to play most every weekend. The first pass we had, I decided to stay at the camp and play basketball.

After the game, it was about one thirty in the morning, and I was climbing into my bunk. The barracks were empty except for me because all the rest of men were gone on the pass. I was almost asleep when I felt somebody crawling into the bed with me. I jumped up out of bed and told a young man he needed to move on to his own bed. He said he was cold and just wanted to get warm. I told him he needed to warn himself somewhere else, and he took my advice and left. I never had any more dealings with that fellow again.

We were told we were going to have a three-day pass in a couple of weeks. I wanted to go to Tulsa, Oklahoma. I don't know why I just wanted to go there. And I had talked about it with some of the other fellows. There was one man whose name was Cook. He was from Kansas City, Kansas, and evidently his family was fairly well-to-do. He was always flush with cash, and liked to gamble. He was kind of a show off but that didn't matter to me. I was going to Tulsa to have a good time.

We checked in at the hotel near the bus station, it was a nice hotel and the first thing Cook did was to tell the bellhop he wanted some action that night. I wasn't in favor of that because I was in Tulsa to have a good time. So I told him I would take a pass on that. I had asked the bellhop when we arrived if they had a good dance hall and Tulsa. He told me the best dance hall in the country was at the Cimarron ballroom. He said I could take a cab from the hotel right down to it.

So after showering and eating supper, I called a cab and went there. It was a massive dance hall and very crowded. They had three dance bands that played continuously. I was in my Army uniform which was an OD uniform (regular military winter uniform, plain, olive drab) for the winter. I couldn't impress anybody with that uniform, and I didn't intend to. I checked around to see what was going on. The dance floor was crowded all the time, and there were tables around the outside of the dance floor.

I spotted a table where young man and his girlfriend were seated. There was another lady with them, but she appeared to be alone. I watched them for a little while, and she got up and danced and they seemed to be having a good time. So I decided I'd go over and see if I could introduce myself to her. She was very pretty and had a gorgeous figure. I told her who I was and what I was doing there, and that I loved to dance.

She said, "I love to dance too, so I said let's get at it." We sure did. We danced just about every dance until about one thirty that morning. She had introduced me to her friends and we were all having a good time. Her friends decided it was time to go eat some breakfast and I just went long. It turned out this man with the other girl was a chef at the country club. So we all drove out to the country club. He took us into the kitchen and made us a big meal of scrambled eggs and bacon and biscuits.

It was nearly four o'clock when we got through eating breakfast and it was time to go home. He suggested he would drop me off at the hotel, and my new friend Laura said, "That won't be necessary; you can take him with me to my apartment. This was on a Friday night and I got to spend the whole weekend with her. We went dancing again Saturday night and had a great time. Sunday afternoon she drove me to the hotel and we said goodbye.

My friend Cook was in the lobby and saw her when we drove up. He asked who she was, and I said, "That was my friend I spent the weekend with. How was your weekend?" He just laughed. We boarded the bus and headed back to camp. Laura drove all the way from Tulsa and spent one night with me there. I don't even remember her last name but I remember Laura and she was just a great date.

CHAPTER 6

Fort Benning, Georgia

I would spend the rest of my time in the service at this location. Johnny Paige was sent to Fort Polk, Louisiana. This post, located in Columbus, Georgia, was a massive post. I arrived by plane on a Sunday, and was to report the next morning to my new company. We were taken by bus to our new billet. On the way, we passed the baseball field and there was some activity going on. I couldn't tell if it was a game or practice, and the bus didn't slow down long enough for me to find out.

I arrived at the billet I was assigned and unloaded my duffel bag. I spotted my friend George Fellows, who I had met at Fort Dix during my eight weeks of basic training. He was assigned to the same company, and we picked out a bunk and unloaded our stuff. The next morning we would have to fall in for Reveille and be accounted for.

Baseball

I headed to the ballfield as soon as I could. The post baseball team was practicing. I introduced myself to the coach and told him I could pitch pretty good. He said, "Get your spikes and sweatpants and let's see what you can do."

I warmed up a pretty long time because I hadn't even thrown a baseball since high school. He said, "Take the mound and throw a few pitches." I did and he said, "I can use you, and if you can get your company commander's permission to leave I'll cut some orders for you."

I took a shower and headed back to the building. When I got

back I told George what the coach had said. The next morning I had to do something about it. After formation I went into the company commander's office, and there was George. He had been assigned as a company clerk. He had made some inquiries as to what I needed to do and told me he could give me an appointment with the company commander.

He did and I presented myself to the company commander and told him what I would like to do. He asked me if that was what I wanted to do and I said yes. He said to clear it with the company clerk and it was okay. I thanked him and told George what he had told me, and George got right on it. My orders were cut the next day. I was given TDY (temporary duty) status. I reported to the coach and started practicing with the baseball team.

I had to go back to the billets each night to sleep. I ate breakfast with the company, and went to practice every day. In about a week, the baseball team had their own quarters and kitchen, so we didn't have to leave to go back to the billets. I had to go back to get my pay once a month. Back then we had to sign when receiving or pay. We had a good baseball team and played all over the third Army area.

There were some other athletes staying in our billets, and I met a boy named Bob Festa, who was from Brooklyn, New York. He was a cross-country long-distance runner, and was in great shape and trained very hard. He had been a company clerk before he got on the team, and was aware of what went on in the companies. He was getting discharged in a few months and did not want to go back to his company when the season was over. He knew pretty much what to do. He was able to get his orders that read "post trainer for the football team." He told me I would need to get some orders also. I played basketball and it was easy for me to get a position on the post-based basketball team. So I got new orders that put me on TDY.

We had to have a place to sleep, and the only place available was under the football stadium, which is not air-conditioned. We got a couple of bunks, mattresses and some linens, and were in business.

We could still eat at our respective companies so we were set for little while. The sleeping conditions under the stadium were horrendous. The mosquitoes at night ate us alive. So I found a friend who was on the football team who knew someone who could get us a large standing fan. I asked if we could get two, and he said maybe.

We got two large standup fans that were very strong. We would set them behind our bunk beds every night before going to sleep, turned them on full blast, and they were so strong that the mosquitoes could not stand the wind. That was the only problem. I was involved in all Fort Benning sports, and made a lot of contacts that were useful.

I used to see Col. Moran from time to time, because he had a son Timmy who played on the Little League basketball team, which I coached. He would ask me how I was doing and I said okay. He worked at the big TIC on the post, which housed the headquarters for everything that went on at Fort Benning.

Grilled Cheese Sandwich

Bob Festa and I were hungry at night when we were living under the stadium, so one Sunday night, we decided we would make us a grilled cheese sandwich. We had gone to the PX that afternoon and bought some sliced cheese and some mayonnaise and bread. We had figured out a way to use Army chairs, the folding metal kind, to toast our sandwiches on. We had two rather large heat lamps which we were going to use to toast the bread. We had two chairs, and we made four sandwiches, two on each chair. We placed them on top of the metal chairs and covered them with the heat lamps. It didn't take very long for the heat lamps to toast the bread.

When we shut the heat lamp off and picked up our grilled cheese sandwiches, much to our surprise, they were covered with OD paint. The heat lamps were so hot they melted the paint on the chairs. Our grilled cheese sandwiches never came into being.

New Set of Orders

Bob Festa told me I would need to get a set of new orders, to keep me on TDY indefinitely. I asked him to write out the orders just like they should be, so he gave me what he thought were good orders to keep me on TDY indefinitely.

The next time I saw Col. Moran, I asked him if he could help me with the orders. He said, "Give me a copy of what you want and I'll get back to you." About two weeks later his son Timmy came by the gym and said his dad wanted to see me. So I went by his house. He lived on post, and that afternoon I stayed just a little while and drank a couple of beers with him. He said, "Here's your new set of orders," and they read just like Bob Festa had put them down. He told me my company commander would receive them in about three days. Now I was pretty set and wouldn't have to go back to the company.

I needed a place to sleep and eat permanently. I could eat at the company, but tried to stay away from there as much as possible. I was afraid some jealous soldiers in my company would try to find out where I was all the time.

I had made a friend on the football team, whose name was Frank Brooks. He was an All-American football player from Georgia Tech. He was very well known in the area and a great football player. His company commander was also a Georgia Tech graduate. He liked Frank very much because he was a good football fan. Frank only had a short time left in the service may be about five months and he liked place, but did not want to go back to his barracks with football season was over. So Col. Ramsey and asked him if there was anything he could help them with. Frank said he needed a place to stay for about five months. Col. Ramsey said he would see what he could do.

The Old Post Gym

There was an old post gym that had a paint shop, a basketball court, and a place where boxers worked out. It also had a large back room that was empty, a good set of showers, and no one on security. When that big back room was fixed up, we had two bunk beds, a television set, a place to get our bedclothes changed once a month. So Frank and I moved in the old post gym. I now had a place to sleep, which was excellent. The place had two telephones, one in the front office and one in the paint shop. We could call all over the post, but not outside the post.

The sergeant in charge of the old post gym had an office in the front where he rarely stayed. His name was RD Baker, and he was a master sergeant with thirty years of service. Most of his service was spent at Fort Benning, and he knew just about everybody in the right places. RD was married and lived on post with his wife, and she used to cook the best homemade southern cooking I ever had. He looked after me like I was his son. He was a master at getting things done.

When a company commander cleared post, he would have to account for all the supplies he had signed for when he took control of the company. Over a period of time, some of the supplies would have disappeared. So they would call RD Baker and say, "Sarge I need so-and-so and so-and-so." They would give him a list of what they needed to fill their supplies.

He would then call other company commanders and find out if any of these things were available or how much longer those commanders would remain. He would manage to swap out items and cover these company commanders' butts. This was a way it worked if you had experience. I was set for place to live and a great set a new orders I had no one to report to, no restrictions on my coming and going. I did not need a pass to get off post so I could leave anytime I wished.

My New Catcher

During baseball season I had a new catcher, who was married and lived off post and had four boys. He was very good and we got to be good friends. I asked him one day what he did when he wasn't playing baseball. He said he worked at the big Martin Army

Hospital. I said, "What you do out there?" He said, "I issue a meal tickets to all the outpatients who are not confined to the hospital." I asked, "How does that work?" He said once a month a new meal ticket was issued to every outpatient. The ticket would be punched when the outpatient went through the cafeteria. Each month the color would change, so there was no fraud.

I asked him how hard it would be for me to get ahold of one of those meal tickets every month. He laughed and said it would be hard for me to get them, but he would be glad to get me one every month. He had several months left to go in the service, and I knew this would be helpful to me. I think I might have given him a dozen new Spaulding baseballs that he really appreciated.

Now I had a place to eat the best food on the post. I could eat three meals a day, one meal a day or all meals a day. Now I could stay away from the company except for payday. Frank had a car I could borrow during the week. He would go home one weekend, and I would make other arrangements for transportation.

We didn't have a whole lot of money and Frank got the bright idea about the poker games the boxers held upstairs. I asked what he had in mind. He said for the first two weeks after payday they came with three or four nights a week. We had the keys to the gym, and could lock it up. Frank said, "Suppose we tell them we'll provide them with some snacks and privacy so they can play poker upstairs. I said, "How will we be getting money from that?" He said, "We'll just cut their pots one percent every night. So we had a cash flow started which helped us both. It wasn't a lot of money but it was better than we had had before.

Basketball Coach

My basketball coach was a second lieutenant, and lived in the basic officers' quarters. He was a really good guy and a fair basketball player. He shared his quarters with another second lieutenant who I had met several times. We used to go have a few beers at night, and visit.

His job was a paymaster for all the patients at Martin Army Hospital. He also was a paymaster for four or five companies. Mine included. He would drive to the Martin Army Hospital with a Jeep and an MP and pay the people in the hospital. They would sign for the pay, and he would return to the barracks to pay off the different companies. I mentioned to him the fact that I was in one of these companies, and he had seen my name on the payroll. I asked him how much trouble it would be for him to swing by the gym upon leaving the hospital and let me sign for my pay. He said it wouldn't be any trouble at all.

So now I had a way to sever all my trips back to the company. I had a place to sleep, a great meal ticket, and a way to get paid. The best part of the deal was George Fellows, my company clerk, had put me up for promotion each time I was eligible. So I got promoted to a specialist fourth class, which gave me more money. I really laid low and played slow. I wanted nobody poking into my business.

Frank was soon going to be discharged and I wanted to keep my quarters safe. So when Col. Ramsey came by one day I asked him about staying there. He thought it would be good for the security of the gym so nothing was done about that.

Golf Clubs

Frank had made enough money off the poker games to buy himself a new set of golf clubs. He sold me his whole set for $30, bag and all. I had never played golf in my life but I thought it was a good idea to have the clubs. Martin Army Hospital is located right on the golf course, where you could sit in the mess hall and watch the golfers play. I'd seen them play several times and thought it would be fun. This was an officers' club golf course exclusively. Being a specialist class 4 I couldn't see how I would ever get to play there.

My pay officer played a lot of golf. He was pretty good too. I mentioned to him I would like to go sometime and ride in the cart with him. He said sure so I had made the rounds with him about half a dozen times. I knew nothing else about golf, so I decided to learn.

In Columbus, Georgia, they had a really nice driving range and a putting surface. I used to go there nearly every day and practice. I putted a lot, and I hit the balls a lot. I started to go to the library, and read up all I could about golf, the rules and etiquette. I now had to find a place to play golf.

The pro at the country club was also on my basketball team off post. We played for a semiprofessional basketball team owned by a man named Jackie Nocera. He was retired from the service and had a big pizza parlor. He also had several other investments and was a good businessman. So I knew the golf pro at the officers' club, and I asked him how hard it would be for me to get to play out there. He said almost impossible since I was not an officer. I said okay, but he added, if I could get a sponsor I might have a chance. Since my orders read "post trainer for all athletic sports at Fort Benning," I thought I just might be able to pull it off.

I approached Col. Moran with the idea. He asked what he could do, and I said he could be my sponsor and send me a letter stating so. He didn't have a problem with that and I presented it to the directors of the officers' club. It didn't take my rank or anything, just my qualifications in post training. I was assigned a locker room and all the privileges of the officers' golf club. I could go by Martin Army Hospital and eat lunch and walk to the golf course to play golf when I wasn't playing ball.

I had a lot of free time to do what I wanted to do and I visited the main post cafeteria four times a week at lunchtime. This is where all the civilian personnel ate lunch. And there were many, many good-looking girls who worked on post. And I had no trouble meeting them and getting dates.

I dated this one young lady who was from Miami. She was a dental technician and work for a really good dentist. I told her I was getting discharged sometime in the next ten months and sure would like to have someone look at my teeth and see if I was okay. It'd been since high school since I'd had any dental work. She got the appointment with the doctor, and he started with a full mouth x-ray and worked on my teeth for about two weeks. I really had some great work done.

Panama City, Florida

I had met this nice young lady at the Newman Club. Her father owned the club. I dated her several times and we got along very well. She wanted me to take her to Panama City, Florida, to go swimming and see the beach. I had heard a lot of things about Panama City and how pretty it was. So I started trying to figure out a way to go. I had mentioned it to RD Baker a couple of times, and he said, "Why don't you go?" I said I'd think about it.

One day he came by and said, "Why don't you take a tent and sleep on the beach?" I hadn't thought of that, but it sounded like a good idea. So I mentioned it to her, and she was excited about going. She had a girlfriend who wanted to tag along. I didn't much go for that idea. RD had gathered up enough supplies for us to stay six days. We had a tent, coolers, food, lanterns, everything you need to camp out, so we made the trip.

We found an obscure location somewhere way down the beach from the main population. The first thing we did was set up our tent and prepare a place for all four of us to sleep that night. When we went back to the car to get the rest of supplies, a sudden thunderstorm came up, and lightning hit so close to where we were it knocked us to the ground. I had a terrific headache for about two hours. We climbed in our tent and stayed there until the weather was better.

The next day we lay around on the beach. RD had provided some soft drinks and some beer. That night we went out dancing and had a great time. We stayed only four days, but that was enough, and we returned to Columbus, Georgia.

The Cousins

I had met these two girls at the cafeteria and found that they were cousins living in a small town in South Alabama. I used to date both of them, and always had a great time. Both of them could really dance and liked to party. We used to go up to Warm Springs, Georgia, where Pine Mountain was located. I found out later this is where President Franklin Roosevelt had his retreat. It was beautiful and there was a big lake there. We used to go up there and picnic stay at night on top of the mountain. It was really beautiful and quiet.

Baseball Trips

The baseball team would travel all over the Third Army area, playing all these different bases. On one trip, we loaded on the bus and headed for Eglin Air Force. Our first stop was to eat lunch somewhere in Florida. There was a nice barbecue place on the right-hand side of the highway so we pulled in the parking lot. We all got out to stretch our legs and went in the place to eat.

We sat down to order and the owner came over and told the coach he was not allowed to serve the black players in the restaurant. They had a place in the back where there were some tables and chairs where they could eat.

I couldn't believe what I was seeing or hearing. In my whole life I had never seen anybody discriminated against. It was terrible. It was my first encounter with racial discrimination. Nobody made much of a fuss about it, and we went on our way.

Playing sports always had some real advantages. When we arrived at Eglin Air Force Base we stayed in some really nice quarters with our own mess hall, where we could order whatever we wanted to eat that was on the menu.

The next day we had to practice in the morning, and that afternoon they had a deep-sea fishing trip for those who wanted to go. I had never been deep-sea fishing and I enjoyed it immensely. That night we went to the club, which had a dance band and plenty of girls. We stayed out till about one o'clock and took the bus back to the quarters.

The next day we were to play the game. I pitched, it was a good game, and we won. We headed back to Fort Benning and we all had a good time. The trip was most memorable to me because I had witnessed something I had never seen, and it made a lasting impression on me.

While back at Fort Benning I had met this basketball player who was from Chicago and his name was Elder. He was a great basketball player, and understudied for Marcus Haynes, who at that time played for the Harlem Globetrotters. He was known to be the best dribbler in basketball at the time. Now Elder had a master's degree and was very well educated. The Tuskegee Institute was a black college in Alabama. He had met a wonderful lady there and dated her regularly. She was studying to get her law degree.

We had a long conversation about the situation several times, and he would tell me how hard he had to work to get his master's. I guess it's why he didn't associate much with people who were not of his intellectual level. We used to play one-on-one and I learned a lot from him. He told me before I got discharged he wanted to take me down to a section of Columbus, Georgia, that was pretty much segregated.

I had never been in that area before. So he took me to a beer joint where I was the only white person in the area. I felt a little bit uncomfortable, but Elder said not to worry. We had a beer and left. In the car on the way back to Fort Benning, he told me he wanted me to see the situation. I did.

Professional Athletes

The post football team and baseball team had several professional players to come through there and play. Just to name a few: Max McGee, quarterback Green Bay Packers; Steve Korcheck, catcher for the Washington Senators; Al Spangler, shortstop; Billy Moran, second baseman. All these guys were great players who I had played with and against.

The most notable player I met while stationed at Fort Benning was Jim Brown. He was the best athlete I had ever seen; he could do any sport and excel. I saw him on the track one day run 100 yard dash, pole vault, shotput, high jump, and he could beat everyone there. Even played a little basketball. He could not shoot great, but he was hell on the backboards. He was also the most arrogant person I had ever met; that part of him I did not like.

Miles Brown, Native Hawaiian

Miles was a sergeant on the Olympic rifle team. He was a small bore champion .22 caliber rifle champion. He was also the best damn ping-pong player I ever saw. We used to go to the service club where they had a great ping-pong table and Miles would take charge. The rule was if you didn't get beat, you could stay on the table, and he never lost. I used to play constantly and got really good at ping-pong but not good enough to beat him. He couldn't play basketball worth a damn but he could shoot and play ping-pong.

Miles and I used to go to the Howard Johnson's in Columbus, Georgia, on Sunday night and order hot fudge cake with vanilla ice cream. We did that quite often. The first time I ever saw Sylvia was at the Howard Johnson's with her friend from Alabama. Both of these girls were very attractive.

Miles had never been to Vermont, and he wanted to go see some snow in the wintertime. So I told him if he wanted to go home with me over Christmas he would have a good place to stay and see all the snow he wanted. So off we went. I didn't need a pass and he did neither, so we drove to Vermont and stayed at 66 Main St.

I had arranged a shooting match at the armory with some of my old friends who were in the National Guard. Billy Landon was one of them. We had it set up for Saturday morning, and we headed towards the armory. Miles had a large gun case that he carried his rifle in. I believe it was called a Swiss Hammerli, a custom-made very expensive .22. When Miles took it out of the case we were all awed by it. We set the targets up and started shooting. It was not hard to see why Miles was on the Olympic team; he was really very good.

I took him everywhere he wanted to go and we saw plenty of snow. He had met my parents and we enjoyed our stay at 66 Main St. the time went by pretty fast, and we headed back to Fort Benning, Georgia. Miles thanked me many times for that trip. We stayed friends as long as I was at Fort Benning and played a lot of ping-pong.

PART 3
COLLEGE, COURTSHIP AND MARRIAGE

CHAPTER 7

Courting Sylvia

As I mentioned earlier I had first seen Sylvia at a Howard Johnson's. Miles and I were eating fudge cake. She was just gorgeous and she was with her girlfriend from Fort Mitchell, Alabama, who was also very good-looking. I had seen her from time to time at a place called the Stop and Tell drive-in. I had never made any contact with her and didn't think much about it.

My basketball coach wanted me to go on a blind date with him and his date, who had a friend. He picked me up and when we went to pick up our dates, much to my surprise his date was Sylvia, and mine was her friend.

I just couldn't take my eyes off her and had a couple of dances with her and found out a little information. She lived in Phenix City, Alabama, which was right across the river. She was a secretary and had a full-time job. I managed to get her telephone number, and the first chance I got I called her. I had to persist for several times before she agreed to go on a date with me. She had some friends who were going on a picnic up to Pine Mountain, Georgia. We cooked hamburgers and hot dogs and drank a few soft drinks. I brought along my ukulele and tried to serenade her but with no success.

On the way back that night I was in the backseat of the car with her and I tried several times to kiss her. Each time I leaned over, she would pop a cigarette in her mouth and say, "Would you give me a light please?"

I really, really liked her and dated her several more times. She knew nothing about sports, but would always go to every game

I played, sit in the stands, and always be there when the game was over.

She had come to Fort Benning to see a baseball game between Paris Island Marines and the Fort Benning soldiers. I was to pitch that game and did. We won two to nothing. After the game was over, off the baseball field I asked her if she liked the game, and she said yes. I told her I had pitched a no-hitter, and she said, "Did you win?" I just chuckled.

Sylvia was engaged at the time I started dating her to a West Point cadet who had given her a ring and was pretty serious about her. I don't believe the feeling was mutual because in a short while she had sent him a letter calling off engagement. From that point on we dated continuously. Every chance I get I would take her out somewhere. She had an automobile, and we would go to the drive-in a lot and just to the drive-in restaurant and have a sandwich. She would drop me off at the old post gym and drive home.

As I stated earlier somewhere, the old post gym had phones but you could not call out on them. She could call in and did so every night after she got home and we talked and talked and talked. The time was drawing near for me to report to the University of Georgia. I really was very serious about marrying Sylvia and I knew she loved me a lot. I thought it would be a good idea for her to meet my parents and go to Vermont. So before school started we talked about making the trip.

Sylvia's Trip to Vermont

I knew I would get a lot of resistance from her father about making this trip. He and I didn't see eye to eye on many things. I had really good allies in her grandmother and her mother. And even her grandfather. So in a couple weeks we were set to go. We headed to Vermont.

We stopped to eat breakfast on the New Jersey Turnpike, early in the morning on the second day. The Howard Johnson restaurant had horseshoe bars where if you were sitting on one end of the horseshoe, you could see right to the next one in front of you.

After breakfast arrived, we were sitting there eating, and Sylvia began to nudge me with her knee. She got my attention and whispered in my ear, "Look over there is a black man sitting with that white lady." I didn't think anything about that, but I realized this was the first time she had ever seen that in her life. Being brought up in the deep South that was a fairly common attitude.

After I paid for our breakfast and got on the road. She and I talked about that a little while, but I was married to her nearly sixty years and she was not prejudiced in any way. She just had never seen that before. We arrived in Ludlow at 66 Main St. and my grandparents were really excited to meet her and my mother also. She was beautiful had a lot of class, and had a really large Southern drawl.

My grandfather just could not get enough of her conversation. My uncle John could hardly wait to get her on the square dance floor and swing her around. So we attended a square dance on Saturday night, and sure enough she saw some of the wildest great swinging she had ever seen. She took it in stride and had a good time. When we left, my grandmother told her to be sure and look after me. They really fell in love with Sylvia.

CHAPTER 8

University of Georgia

I had made a lot of friends playing basketball and baseball outside of Fort Benning. One of the teams I played for was a semipro basketball team, sponsored by a man named Jackie Noceras. He was a retired military, from New Jersey. He had several interests besides the pizza place and loved basketball. We received no pay but carte blanche to all his pizza parlors, which was pretty nice; we could get a cold beer and a pizza on a date anytime. Playing outside of Fort Benning, I had attracted some attention from some Georgia alumni. One of them was a large real estate man who was very wealthy, and another owned a large clothing store in downtown Columbus, Georgia. The real estate man was responsible for my full scholarship to the University of Georgia.

When Sylvia and I arrived back in Phenix City from Vermont, I had about three days before I had to report to school. Having been in the service for the last three years, I had no clothes to wear the college. My real estate friend who had got my scholarship was aware of this, and he called me down to his office and said, "John, go over to the clothing store and they'll fix you up."

I didn't have any money devoted to clothes. I went around to the clothing store, and sure enough the owner was waiting for me at the front door. He said, "Come on back, John, and we'll fix you up for school. This was a first-class clothing store and the clothes he fixed me up with were the best money could buy. I told him I didn't know when I'd be able to pay him for the clothes. He said, "Don't worry about it; it's all been taken care of." So I headed off to school.

Freshman Year

There were very few Yankees at University of Georgia, and I had to adapt to a totally new environment and lifestyle. Most of the students at University of Georgia were younger than I was. I fit in pretty quickly, probably because I was on scholarship. All the athletes lived in the same dorm. We had our own cafeteria downstairs in the basement and had the best food on the campus. There were two athletes to each room, and my roommate was from Columbus, Georgia. His name was Gordon Darrah.

Football is king at the University of Georgia and all the other Southeastern Conference schools. Some of these football players were pretty rowdy but not dangerous, just a little wilder than the other athletes. I learned to accept that and get along with no problem.

I still had my Yankee lingua. One day in my English class, we were reading about Huckleberry Finn. Each student was required to stand and read some part of this story. My time came, and I was reading along at a pretty good clip. I came across the word I had never seen before, and it went something like this. Huckleberry Finn was sitting under a persimmon tree. I had never seen the word persimmon before so I pronounced it piscimen. All the students began to laugh, and the teacher corrected me right away and told me how to say it. I never mispronounced that word again.

Basketball Practice

We practiced basketball six and a half days a week, only half a day on Saturday. Phenix City, Alabama, was a pretty good ways away and in order to get there to see Sylvia I had to hitchhike. I would leave right after basketball practice on Saturday about twelve thirty and hit the road. Most times I would probably get there about six thirty or seven o'clock that evening. I would have to leave late Sunday afternoon to go back to school. I always could get a ride back with some students who lived in Columbus, Georgia. That didn't give me much time to visit with Sylvia, but I would go sometimes.

My Only Other Date

This new environment that I was in at the university was totally different for me. I had never seen so many good-looking women in my whole life. And as I looked around, I began to wonder if Sylvia was a girl I wanted to spend the rest of my life with. I decided I'd better find out pretty quick, so I picked the best-looking girl on campus, the most popular and the one who had the best figure. I asked her out and she accepted. She was very nice and I had a good time.

That date proved to me that not any girl could touch Sylvia in my mind. I had a good time, but it just wasn't the real deal. So when I got back to our room that night, I called Sylvia and I told her, "Sugar, I want to marry you.

She said, "Okay, but you have to talk to my dad first to get his permission."

Her dad and I never did agree on many subjects, so I dreaded the thought. The first chance I got when I went back to Phenix City to see Sylvia, I planned to speak to her father. It was a Saturday, and he was sitting on the front porch smoking a cigarette. There was no one else there but him and me. I got up the courage and walked up to him, and said, "Mr. Wilson, I want to marry your daughter."

There were no words exchanged, but he let out a big grunt, got up and walked into the house. I took that as a yes. Fortunately for me, her grandmother and her mother really liked me. Her grandmother was a bridal consultant at one of the big department stores in Columbus, Georgia, called Kirvens. I went back to school, and they made all the plans.

School was soon to get out for the Christmas holidays. So we picked the date. December 27, 1959. This is two days after Sylvia's birthday; she was born on Christmas day. The wedding was to take place at St. Patrick's Church in Phenix City, Alabama. This was the Catholic Church. I was Catholic and Sylvia was Methodist but that did not create a problem.

CHAPTER 9

Newlyweds

I headed back to school and the basketball season was fully underway. It was a short time before Christmas break, and we got married. It was a bad rainy day but a great day. We loaded up her Chevrolet with all her belongings. A few utensils and things we would need when we got to our apartment. We looked like the Beverly hillbillies when we left town. We had an iron and ironing board laid on top of all the stuff in the backseat, and it was quite a sight.

I had rented an apartment from this widow lady not far from campus, and paid the rent so we had a place to stay when we got to Athens, Georgia. I believe we had about $125 in cash, and decided to drive all the way to Athens so as not to spend our money.

About sixteen miles from Athens there was a little town called, Winder, Georgia. It had rained almost all the way up to that point. I thought I heard something clank on the back of the car, so I stopped. I got out and walked around the back and didn't see a thing. So I got back in and started the car and started to pull out on the highway. I was stuck. The ground was really soft, and I didn't know till later on, that the highway department had released water into some culvert along the side of the road that week.

So there we were sixteen miles from touchdown. There was a farmhouse across the highway on the other side of the road, so I decided that was my only chance this late at night. I told Sylvia to sit tight and I would walk over there and see if I could get some help.

I knocked on the door, and the farmer came and said, "What do you want?" I told him I had just got married and was on the way to

Athens to my apartment and was stuck. He told me then why the ground was so soft. It didn't help my conscience any but I asked him if he could help me try to get out. He said he would so he got dressed and came over there but we could not get out of the mud.

I still had my blue suit on, and Sylvia was wearing a long white coat. I was covered in mud and soaking wet. The farmer explained I could call the wrecker service in Winder, Georgia, and they would come and pull me out, so I did. They charged me $58, so our cash was getting low.

We drove on to the apartment and I was really cold and wet. I had to wake up the landlady, and she knew who I was because I had paid her the rent in advance. She took one look at me and said, "Lord have mercy, what happened to you?"

I told her about getting stuck she said, "That's terrible; y'all get in the house." So we unloaded and went upstairs to the apartment, made up the bed got into our pajamas started to get warm.

It was Saturday morning, and all the food we had was to snacks her mother had made us when we left Phenix City. So we had to go buy some groceries. My scholarship provided for a stipend for married students living off campus. I had a check waiting for me at my mailbox at school. I went by and picked it up. I don't remember the exact amount but it was less than $200. Sylvia and I had never shopped for groceries and knew nothing about setting up house-keeping. We went by the 7-11 store and bought a few things. When we unloaded what little bit we had, I remember looking in this huge pantry and only seeing a bottle of ketchup a loaf of bread and some mustard. I thought to myself, my goodness that's not much. But any-way we made out pretty good.

It was still Christmas holiday and school was closed until after the first of the year. So we had a few days to ourselves. My first class began at ten a.m., so we didn't have to get up too early. Basketball practice resumed, and class resumed.

Sylvia found a job right away as a bookkeeper for the Eli Witt cigar and tobacco company. She had to be at work at seven thirty a.m. It was still winter and cold in the morning. Since I didn't have to get up to go to class until ten o'clock, I would sometimes stay in the bed and she would leave for work. We began to adjust to our new lifestyle and in the next few weeks went by pretty fast.

One evening, Sylvia had gotten lost on the way home from work and was very upset. She told me that night after supper she wanted to go back to Phenix City and stay with her mother. I got pretty upset about this, but I said, "Okay, you can leave in the morning."

Morning came in she had calmed down some and said she was sorry she didn't really want to go back. So we finished out the year at school. We went back to Phenix City for the summer. We stayed with her parents, and I needed a job. I found one right away as a salesperson selling Collier encyclopedias. I had never done anything like that, but I was willing to try.

Encyclopedia Salesman

My training consisted of three days in the local office, learning the sales pitch and two more days with the supervisor in the field observing. The following week the supervisor took me to a place in Columbus, Georgia, where a lot of military people lived. I had a briefcase with my materials for selling the encyclopedias. He dropped me off at about six thirty in the evening and said he would pick me up about nine thirty.

There I was, getting ready to make my first sales pitch. I got up the courage and knocked on my first door, and the family let me in. I explained to them what I was doing and asked if they would be interested in buying a set of encyclopedias for the children. They said, "Let's see what you got." I made my sales pitch, and got my first sale. I didn't want to push my luck and was very excited. I stayed in the house a long time and they had fed me some cookies and milk.

It was getting late in the evening and I knew my supervisor would be by to pick me up soon. So I went out in the street and walked maybe a block, sat down on the curb and waited. He picked me up and said, "How did you do?" I told him I made a sale. He was excited for me, and said, "I think you're going to make it."

I did sell encyclopedias all that summer, and I made some good money and we were able to pay Sylvia's parents for staying with them. Sylvia had managed to save some of that money to help us next year at school.

Towards the end of the summer, we would go out of town to sell these encyclopedias. One trip was to Albany, Georgia, which was just a few miles from Columbus. The supervisor dropped me off in an area where there were a lot of families whose men worked for the railroad. So the first door I knocked on, they were eating supper and asked me to come in and sit down. I did and after they finished supper, we went into the living room, and I told them basically about the program. The lady said, "Wait a minute," and she went and called two of her neighbors. They were interested in listening to my proposal. So I pitched all three families at the same time and sold all three.

I was excited and went back outside. There were some boys playing catch and I started to play with them. It wasn't long before my supervisor came by to pick me up. As he stopped, a police car pulled over. We had not gotten a permit to solicit within the city limits of Albany, Georgia. So off we went to the local jail. The supervisor convinced them to take a check for our bond. So we left Albany, and the following week my supervisor left town. I just assumed this check was good so that they wouldn't be after him. I submitted my three sales that week and was paid. It was my last job for them.

CHAPTER 10

Phenix City, Alabama

Temper Tantrum

I had come home one day right after lunch, and had some very important information to tell Sylvia. I don't even remember what it was. When I came in she was talking on the phone with her friend Eleanor. I said, "Baby I got something I need to tell you." She just ignored me and kept on talking. Several times I tried to get her attention and she just ignored me and kept talking.

I finally lost my temper and pulled the phone right off the wall. I said, "Dammit, listen to me." The next day the phone repair man came and asked what happened to the phone. She told him, "My husband lost his temper pulled it off the wall." He cautioned her to try not to make me mad.

Sylvia's Pregnant

Just before we started back to school, we found out Sylvia was expecting a baby. She decided to stay with her family instead of returning to school with me. I had a full scholarship and didn't want to jeopardize that so I returned to school without her. Since I still was in married status, I had to rent a room and I did. Things are going along pretty good in school and basketball. I knew Sylvia was in good hands with her mother in Phenix City.

The morning of November 27, 1961, her brother Butch called me early in the morning and said Sylvia was in labor and on her way to the hospital. So I got the old Chevrolet and headed for Phenix City. Actually she was in the hospital in Columbus, Georgia.

When I arrived at the hospital, nothing had happened so far, and she was having a difficult time with her labor. The doctor came out at one point and told me she was having some complications. He didn't say what they were, and I said "Well, I don't want to hear about the complications. I want you to go in there and take care of her."

He did and a couple hours later my first son was born. John Wilson Barnard. November 27, 1961.

Tough Cookie

Johnny was a pretty little fella, and we were able to take him home a few days later. He developed some problems, later diagnosed as pyloric stenosis. This was not uncommon in male children. He had to have surgery to correct it when he was only six weeks old. Due to his problem he was not getting the proper nourishment because he couldn't keep his food down, so he wasn't all that strong when he had surgery. He was a tough cookie at only six weeks, and now at nearly sixty years of age, he's still a tough cookie.

He came out of the surgery okay, but with me in school and Sylvia at home with her mother, it was a hard time for her and the baby. He had to have special formula, and lots of TLC. His medical bills were mounting up and I was quite concerned about that as we had no insurance. The basketball team at this time was traveling all over playing conference teams. I called nearly every night to see how he and Sylvia were getting along. He seemed to be doing just fine.

Trip to LSU and Baton Rouge, and Bourbon Street

The Georgia basketball team traveled to Baton Rouge to play LSU. We flew in and it was very bad weather, cold, which was unusual for New Orleans. We all stayed at the Hilton near the airport. We played LSU the next day in an arena sometimes called the house that Bob Pettit built. He was an alumnus of LSU and went on to become a super professional basketball player.

We only had one game and played it the next day. The weather was still pretty bad and we went back to the hotel and spent the night. We could not fly out due to the snow and ice. Three of us got the idea we needed to go down to Bourbon Street. So we waited till about ten o'clock that night, hitched a ride and down we went. I mentioned earlier that I wondered what New Orleans would be like. And it was wonderful, lots of good entertainment, good music and wonderful sites.

The three of us ended up that evening at a place called Pat O'Brien's. This club was noted for a drink called a hurricane. It was a mixture of a lot of alcohol in the big tall glass that had Pat O'Brian's name on the side. The stage had two piano players, one on each side of the stage, and the MC was in the middle. He came over to our table and said, "You boys look like you're in college." We said we sure were, and he said, "I could get you a few free drinks if you just follow my lead."

He told us when he mentioned the name of a college and started singing their fight song, to stand up. "Someone will buy you a hurricane." We did and every time we did, we had several rounds of drinks. We were feeling very well when we got back to the hotel about four o'clock in the morning. The coach had pulled a bed check and found us missing earlier that evening. So he was waiting for us and we paid the consequences. At our next basketball practice we probably ran fifty laps, but it was worth because we did have a great time.

The Gator Bowl

In Jacksonville, Florida, every year there is a big contest called Gator Bowl. Football was a highlight, but there was also a basketball tournament at the same time. Each participant in the tournament received a beautiful watch with a picture of a gator on the inside. I kept my watch for a long time. Somehow I lost mine over the years, I don't remember when, but it was a beautiful watch.

Extra Money

Sylvia and the baby were getting along pretty well, and I had to finish up that year at Georgia. I couldn't get home every weekend, so I played golf at the country club which was free. The ninth hole at the country club had a large pond in front of the tee box. You had to drive over the pond onto the fairway and then onto the green. There were probably thousands of golf balls in the pond. One of the football players from Stone Mountain, Georgia, decided we might be able to dive for some of those golf balls, clean them up and sell them for about fifty cents apiece.

So we had a plan for when the weather was warm enough for us to do it. Our plan was to go out there at night, park the car in the woods and go down to the pond. Sounded like a pretty good idea so we picked the date. Three of us including a football player, a boy from Columbus, Georgia, and another guy from New York bought a couple of six packs and stripped down to our shorts. We each had a knitted laundry bag which we could tie around our neck and use to hold the golf balls.

We had been there about an hour and of course we were having a good time drinking beer and diving for golf balls. The football player cautioned us about making too much noise. He said this several times. About eleven o'clock that evening, a loud voice boomed out, "Come out of there with your hands up."

Oh my God we got caught. I was married and I knew damn well that I'd probably get thrown out of school. Flashlights were shining on the pond so I stayed close to the cart path where they couldn't see me. On the other side of the cart path it was very nasty and marshy. I decided my best chance not to be discovered was diving into the pond and staying close to the bank hidden. I did and then I heard a shotgun go off. Pellets were hitting the other pond and I hunkered down. I waited a long time for things to quiet down.

The guy from New York had taken off running down the golf course in his underwear, and I didn't know where the other guy was.

101

So after a while I crawled out of the pond, looked around, crawled on my hands and knees on the cart path and over to the fairway. Still no activity and no signs of anybody, so I got up and ran to the woods and headed for the car.

As I approached the car, I heard a lot of laughing going on. This was some kind of a gag that the football player had dreamed up to scare the hell out of us. He did. The other guy and the football player and two of his buddies drove us back to the dorm. I was filthy, and I took a shower. While I was in the shower, I discovered I had several leeches on me from being in a nasty pond. I pulled them off, and the guys were still laughing and talking about how we got scared.

In about thirty minutes, the guy from New York came into the dorm in his underwear, and he was mad as hell. There wasn't much else said that evening but somehow we had to get him back for this.

Medical Bills

Johnny had to have special formula, and he was slowly progressing. We didn't have insurance so we had to charge all of our stuff at the local drugstore, which was owned by a Georgia man and he carried us for long time. This was weighing very heavily on Sylvia and our minds. We talked about it and I prayed about it. I couldn't let the situation continue.

So I went to the baseball coach Mr. Whatley and told him that I was going to leave school and give up my scholarship. I told him why, and he understood, but he said maybe we could work something out. I didn't go for that, and I left school that year and never went back. It was a hard decision, but it was a good decision.

PART 4

PROFESSIONAL AND FAMILY LIFE

CHAPTER 11

Learning to be a Father and Husband

Johnny's Trip to Vermont as a Baby

Sylvia and Johnny and I had flown into Rutland, Vermont, on one particular trip. This was a very small airport and sometimes dangerous. The trip on the big plane to Boston was okay. When we began to approach the Rutland airport, the plane seemed to drop out of the sky. I was holding Johnny with one hand and my other hand was on the armrest. Luggage began to fall over the place and we began dropping fast.

I remember hitting my head on the overhead rack and my seatbelt came loose. The plane was being battered around by crosswinds below the mountain range. Once the plane had stabilized, the pilot said we were going to bypass this airport and go on to Burlington to be safe. Burlington was about 100 miles farther north, and we landed safely there.

They provided us with transportation back to the Rutland airport where we had a car waiting for us, and we proceeded to the 66 Main St. in Ludlow. This was Johnny's first trip, and he was so young I don't think he remembers much of the trip if any. We got to spend time with my family, and they got to see little Johnny boy.

Pat had taken Johnny to Lake Ninevah, where there was a good brook to fish in. He held Johnny in his arms and waded in the creek and took him fishing. Pat was a good man. He was always good to me and I spent a lot of time with him outdoors.

Johnny's Trips to the Emergency Room

Johnny's grandmother was taking reducing pills. Johnny got ahold of the bottle and swallowed a bunch of them one day. He was just a little baby and he was still in his crib. He got so hyper, I bet he asked me a thousand times, "Wash my ball, Daddy, wash my ball," over and over and over. We finally had to take him to the emergency room at the Columbus hospital. We told them what happened and they immediately gave him suppository.

It took about eighteen hours for the suppository to override the stimulation from the reducing pills. He finally went to sleep and slept all the next day and through that night. He was okay so we got to take him home the next morning.

When I went out to the parking lot to get the car, I noticed our German Shepherd lying on the pavement by the car. He had seen us take Johnny in the car and followed us all the way to the hospital. It was all pavement, and his paws were pretty injured. I loaded him in the backseat and went and got Johnny and Sylvia. We went home and I doctored his paws up. He was so happy when he saw Johnny and everything seemed to get back to normal.

One other time Johnny had got ahold of one of my fishing corks and somehow got it caught in his lower lip. Sylvia thought he got a fish hook in there because the cork would not come off his lip. We took him to the emergency room and the attendant just laughed. He just mashed the end of the cork and it came loose.

My First Job

I went to work for the Prudential Insurance Company as a salesman, and I did pretty good. We finally had some money coming in and were able to pay on our bills at the drugstore. We moved into an apartment not too far from Sylvia's mother's place and stayed there for little while. I was to attend the company convention in New Orleans, Louisiana. While I had already been there one time, I told Sylvia I was really looking forward for us to go there together.

We stayed at the Jung Hotel, which was near Bourbon Street. We took in all sights and saw a good show at the Roosevelt Hotel. Several of us attended this show, and we had a big long table right down in the front. They had set us up to eat, and the table had big tall water glasses. I believe they were goblets. While the show was going on, one of the guys with us was leaning his head towards the right trying to get a real good look at the dancers. He inadvertently let his ear fall into the goblet of water. When he felt the water he jumped up out of his chair and was surprised. We all got a pretty good chuckle out of that but no harm was done. We had a good time at the convention and went back to Columbus, Georgia.

I was pretty much on my own every day and had to report to the office in the morning. This free time wasn't very good for me because began to pick up some bad habits. I started playing pool, a little poker, staying out too late. I wasn't very motivated to succeed; I just wanted to have fun.

We had moved to a nice house in Columbus, Georgia. Sylvia was staying with Johnny and he was doing much better. Sylvia was pregnant and our little Michael came along. I was not handling my responsibility very well, and my outside activities were consuming most of my time. I started playing golf. The city golf course was located off the highway in Columbus and had a large putting green under the streetlights. Sometimes when we finished playing golf, we would stay out there putt.

We gambled a lot, which I could not afford, and Sylvia warned me if I didn't straighten up she would take the boys and leave. I didn't think she'd ever do that, and boy was that a mistake. One day after playing golf, we started putting and having a few beers. While all these men I was playing with were businessmen, and were financially secure, I was good enough to beat them, and I knew it. So I stayed and putted all night. When we finally finished it was about seven thirty in the morning.

I headed home and stopped and had a little breakfast. When I got home the car was gone, and I wondered why. The door was locked so

I took my keys and went in the kitchen. Boy was I surprised. There was one chair at the kitchen table. All the furniture in the house was gone, Sylvia was gone and the kids were gone. The only thing left was the dog in the backyard. I realized then that when she told me she would take the children away and leave, she meant it. But I didn't think this would last very long.

Two days later, I realized that I had to move out and find me a room. I did and I tried to find out from her mother where she was living, with no success. Sylvia had gotten a job and was working in downtown Columbus. I saw the car by chance one day and waited around to see her come out. I walked over to her. I don't even remember what I said. She paid me no attention. She just got in her car and drove off.

I went back to my room that I had rented wondered what in the world would I do. I had not eaten well because I didn't have much money. My landlady was so stingy she even got after me about stealing a banana. Sylvia evidently thought I was looking poorly and mentioned it to her mother. Her mother mentioned it to her grandmother, and I got a call at work in the morning. It was Friday, she invited me over to dinner Sunday. And I gladly accepted.

Her grandmother and grandfather lived in a nice home. They both had good jobs. I was probably starving to death and ate like a pig. After dinner, they sat me down in the living room. They had a heart-to-heart talk with me and told me I could come stay with them provided I straightened up.

By then I was ready to do anything because I really missed Sylvia and the children. So I stayed with them about three weeks, ate regular meals, and started doing better physically. I wasn't doing worth a hoot at my job so I quit.

Liberty National Insurance Company

I ran into a friend I had worked with at Prudential. He said they were looking for some salesmen, and I should go to the Liberty National office and apply for a job. So I did and this was the best thing that it ever happened to me in my whole life as far as work. I interviewed for the job and I knew my credit report was terrible, but the manager looked at me and said, "I'm going to give you a chance."

Monday morning I was on the job, he submitted my application to the home office in Birmingham, Alabama, and they totally rejected it. They told him I was not eligible to be hired, but he said, "It's too late; he's already on the job."

Liberty National was in a downtown area that consisted of all businesses. The manager thought I might do very well down there because I had a good education. They trained their agents very well and I had a great supervisor. His name was B.B. White. He introduced me to all the policyholders we had downtown. Most of them were clerks, ladies who worked in the stores.

I got the hang of it pretty quick. After about six months I was leading the district. In the meantime, I had gone to Sylvia begging for forgiveness, and she accepted me back. We rented a little house not too far from her mother and father, and her mother took care of the children. It was a nice little house with a screened-in porch and a good place for our dog. The dog was a German Shepherd, a stray we had found going through the garbage, and he was very protective of the children.

The Dog

I stated earlier how protective the dog was of the children, and he was especially protective of Michael. One Sunday morning real early, the paper delivery man knocked on our door and said, "Mr. Barnard, your son is up on the highway with that dog."

"I said oh my God he must've gotten out of his crib and got up there and waddled up to the highway."

The deliveryman said he tried to get Michael into his car but the dog would not let him come near Michael. So I put on my pants and shirt and shoes. Michael and the dog hadn't gone very far, and I could see them plodding along. The dog was on the outside keeping him from going in the road. I called out to Michael, and the little rascal turned around and started walking back towards me, the dog was right by his side. I picked Michael up and we went back to the house with no further incident. That German Shepherd stayed really close to Michael most of the time.

Terrible Accident
Sylvia and I and the kids had left to go to the store that day. I had shut the dog up in the house so she wouldn't follow us as she sometimes liked to do. We were not gone very long, maybe a couple of hours. When we arrived back home, I noticed one of the panes on the glass door to the porch was busted. I told Sylvia to stay in the car with the children. I went around and unlocked the front door, and there was blood all over the place. The dog did not come to me as he normally would so I turned and told Sylvia to keep the children in the car.

I walked through the house and could see the blood by the glass door on the porch, and the trail of blood leading to the children's bedroom. When I walked in the door, the German Shepherd was lying between the two beds with blood all over the place. He was dead and had evidently bled to death.

I walked back towards the porch and try to get some idea of what had happened. I saw where he had busted out the pane in the glass door. He got his head out, but couldn't get the rest of his body out so he backed up. When he did, he turned his head from side to side. There was one jagged piece of glass on the bottom of the pane. He must've cut his jugular vein twisting his head from side to side.

I called the veterinarian and asked him to come by the house to see what had happened. He concurred with my story and took the dog with him. In the meantime Sylvia had taken the children to her mother's. We left them with their grandmother and went back to the house to clean it up. It was terrible.

I called the landlord and told him what it happened he came by and saw we had cleaned the house up. I told him that we would have to move because I couldn't bring the children back in that house again. He understood.

A New Home

We found us another house not too far from Sylvia's mother's as she kept the children during the day while we were at work. The Phenix City Country Club was right on my way to work not too far from the house. I started going by and playing a little golf from time to time and as always I couldn't seem to do anything in moderation. One afternoon about one thirty, I was sitting on the big deck on top of the clubhouse drinking a beer. I looked over towards the road and saw Sylvia coming down the road in her car. I was surprised hoped nothing was wrong.

She drove to the parking lot, opened the door to the car and let both my boys out. I walked to the side of the deck and I heard her say to them they should tell Daddy to go get a motel or come home. Both of them were pretty young and they came running towards the clubhouse and up the stairs and calling me Daddy Daddy Daddy. As you can see from this incident my wife Sylvia didn't mess around. I loaded the children up in the car and went home.

My golfing days were over temporarily, but somehow I picked up another bad habit. There was a little snack bar and pool hall combined in downtown Columbus. They made the best chili dogs of anywhere around and I would occasionally go in there and have one. One day I was in there and got up and went towards the back of the counter and saw the pool hall.

There were several tables and it was a large place. In the very front there was what was called a snooker table. I had never seen anybody play snooker and knew nothing about. So I got a chair and watched them play for a little while. You got it. I was so fascinated with how much skill it took to play snooker, I soon was playing regularly getting better every time I played.

There was always gambling on the snooker table and soon I was involved. I got where I stopped by the pool hall every night to shoot snooker and gamble. Sometimes I wouldn't get home till eleven o'clock at night. Sylvia used to really get on to me and pleaded with me to stop. One evening about nine o'clock I was shooting snooker, and I was about to take my shot, when I heard this voice say, "Are you winning any money, sugar?"

I dropped my pool stick turned around knowing good and well who was speaking in that sweet voice. She grabbed me by the arm and waltzed me right on out of the pool hall. I think this was the only time in my sixty years of marriage to Sylvia that I ever heard her use foul language. She got her nails into my biceps and uttered the words, "You son of a bitch." Her next words were for me to follow her home in my car. I did. When we got home she had a few choice words for me, and said if I did not quit she would take the children and leave. That was the last time I ever played snooker.

Something Had to Change

The next morning after not getting much sleep that night, I wondered what in the world was going to happen to us. That morning I got up extra early and headed to the office. I knew the office would not be open so I had some time to kill. I sat in the car for a few minutes, and something happened I started the car up and headed toward the Catholic church.

That early in the morning there was no one around church except me. I knelt down and started to cry. I started to pray, asking the Lord to help me get on the right track and stay on it. I stayed there a pretty good while and then went to the office. I felt a lot better, so I went to work. I continued this process of going to church every morning, and making the same request: Please help me.

Each day began to get better and better for me. I had a complete turnaround. I continued the routine for forty-five days. I never did tell anyone about this is, I was so ashamed of my past. It was not long before I was leading the district. I had changed my habits completely. After about a year and a half, I was promoted to a sales manager in my district of Columbia, Georgia.

We were not on computers at that time and Thursday evenings I would not get home until sometime after eleven o'clock. But still Sylvia didn't mind that at all because I was really working hard and we were making a lot of headway.

St. Patrick's Church
We had become very active in the church and my two boys were altar boys. Both of them attended St. Patrick's school and were doing very well. Father Conroy was our priest and he was an excellent one. Several months went by and we continued to do well. Sylvia asked me that morning in church to see if she could speak to Father Conroy. I said yeah. She said she wanted to talk to him after church. So she did. She had made up her mind to join the church all by herself with no prodding from any of us. She did join the church, took instructions and was confirmed by the bishop in Mobile, Alabama.

Sunday Dinner at Grandma's
Sylvia's mother always used to fix Sunday dinner for us. We had just gotten home from church, and Sylvia's mother a called. She was all upset and crying. We loaded up in the car and went down to the house. I told children to stay in the car. Sylvia got out and saw her mother in the backyard very upset. Her face was very red and she was crying. I told her to get in the car with the children and I went in the house.

Sylvia's dad was sitting in his favorite chair and I confronted him about the situation. He didn't have a word to say to me so I went back out to the car and asked Sylvia's mother what happened. She told me about him verbally abusing her until she ran out into the backyard. I really didn't know at that time Sylvia's daddy had a severe drinking problem I found that out later.

I went into the house and confronted him about the situation. He acted like nothing ever happened so I reached down and grabbed him out of his chair, slammed him up against the wall. I told him that if he ever mistreated Catherine again I would beat the daylights out of him and then I mildly pushed him back down in the chair and we left. There were no more incidents after that that I knew about.

Sylvia's dad had a drinking problem for most of his life. He was very smart and had a lot of talent if he could leave the whiskey alone. Sylvia and I eventually bought the house that they were living in so they would always have a place to stay.

Incident with the Boys

The children were at their grandmother's playing outside and coming in and out of the back door. Johnny had somehow managed to unscrew the eye that the hook went into on the screen door and swallowed it. We rushed him to the emergency room where they took an x-ray. We called Dr. Warr who was our family doctor and he rushed right on over to see about Johnny. He showed us the x-rays and sure enough you could see the eye on the screw plain as day in his gut.

He said, "Well I'm not going to try anything right now but I want you to take him home and give him plenty of bread and cheese. He said if he hasn't passed it by tomorrow evening I'll probably have to do surgery."

He wasn't in any pain or anything so we took him home and got the potty chair out and explained what the situation was to him. So we started feeding him lots of bread and lots of cheese and just waited. The next morning about eight thirty we heard him hollering, "Mama Mama Mama, I see it I see it I see it." And sure enough he had passed it that morning when he had a bowel movement. No harm done, but that could've been very serious.

Oven Cleaner

Somehow when Johnny and Mike were at Catherine's playing around, Johnny got ahold of a bottle of oven cleaner. He proceeded to take the cap off and take a swallow. Oven cleaner has a lot of lye in it and it is extremely dangerous. We rushed him over to the emergency room in Columbus, and they proceeded to pump his stomach out.

We had waited out in the waiting room and finally they came out and said we could go back and see him. He had this tube running down into his stomach pumping it out and he was sound asleep. The doctor said that was good sign that he didn't have any damage and once again no serious problem, but it could've been.

Christmas Tree Shopping

The company I worked for Liberty National insurance had their Christmas party at the country club at Fort Benning, Georgia. We took the entire day off Friday to play golf, eat a lot of good oysters and seafood, and drink quite a bit. I had ridden with somebody else to the party so I wasn't worried too much about getting home. About four thirty or five o'clock in the evening the party broke up and one of the guys gave me a ride home.

I had promised both the children I would take them to buy him a Christmas tree that Friday night. I was not in very good shape to do any Christmas shopping but they were excited and I didn't want to let them down. I remembered that day when I was a little boy and my daddy let me down and I never forgot it. So I got Sylvia to drive us to the Christmas tree lot, and we proceeded to try to pick out a big nice tree.

We found one I liked and I insisted that we buy. We did and took it home. I told the children we would decorated it the next day. So I flopped into bed, mission accomplished. The next morning bright and early both the children were of shaking my leg saying, "Come on, Daddy we're going to decorate the tree." I said okay. I cut some two by fours and made a good stand for it and we got it upright.

It was a total disaster. The tree had very little branches on one side and was crooked. We were all so disappointed, especially me. I said, "Well let's trash the tree and go get another one." So off we went back to the lot and this time I let the children pick out the one they wanted and it was a really nice tree. We took it back home and decorated it and all had a lot of fun doing it.

Michael's Sleeping Habits

Michael never liked to sleep in his bed all night. Sometime in the night he would wake up, take his blanket and pillow and lie on the rug somewhere in the bedroom. So when we checked on him and opened the door we had to be very cautious not to hit them in the head. I would tuck in both the boys at night when I was home early, and little Michael would look up at me and say, "Sweet dreams, I love you, Daddy."

"Sweet dreams, I love you, Daddy" is on his headstone at the cemetery.

The Trip to Florida

I had just purchased a new Buick LeSabre about three weeks earlier. Summer had arrived and we were getting off fairly early on Friday. This particular Friday I decided maybe we ought to take the children and go to Florida for the weekend. So when I got home, I told Sylvia to round up the boys and bring them into kitchen. When I asked them how they'd like to make a trip to Florida, they both were excited so we packed the car and off we went.

We spent the first night in Florida somewhere I don't remember exactly, but the next day we went to the Ross Allen reptile farm. I believe that was the name, but I might be mistaken. They had alligators and snakes and all kinds of wildlife there. We witnessed a man going in the ring with an alligator and turning it on its back. It was amazing he said that once the alligator was on its back and spine, he was temporarily paralyzed.

We also saw one of the attendants milk a rattlesnake. The children were just overwhelmed and so was I. We also saw several rattlesnakes in a cage and the attendant walked in there with big boots on to protect his legs. He had a metal hook and he would walk among the rattlesnakes and aggravate them and you could hear those rattles just make an all kinds of racket.

He finally took a balloon out of his pocket and blew it up and tied it to the end of the hook he said, "Now, ladies and gentlemen, I want you to see how fast the snakes can strike." He maneuvered the balloon down in front of one of the snakes. It was rattling real loud and pretty soon the balloon popped. I never did see the snake strike, and the children said they didn't see it either. That's how fast these rattlers could strike.

We had a great time there and then continued on down to Silver Springs. This is where they had glass bottom boats that you could tour and see all the underwater life. It was really a fascinating trip. When we were about to dock after our excursion, the guide reached in his pocket and threw out some coins on top of the glass. Of course we all knew he was looking for some tips.

Michael had seen him do it and he said, "What did you do that for?" Everybody laughed, and I told him I would explain it to him later, and I did. He said, "Why didn't he just ask for a tip?" I said I didn't know.

We then drove up the coast to Fort Walton and Panama City, Florida. We got a little bit farther up where it wasn't so crowded and we booked a room at the Hilton that night. They had a wonderful swimming pool and a really good waterfront. Johnny loved the beach, and Michael liked the pool. We just hung around that day and had a great time, and went out for supper and then to bed. We checked out the next morning and headed back towards home. It was really a nice trip; we all had a good time.

Bloody Marys
Sylvia and I went to Panama City and Fort Walton Beach several times. One of the highlights of our trip was she would make us some Bloody Marys in advance. When we would approach Fort Walton and Panama City, she would lean over to me and say, "It's time for us to have a Bloody Mary." We always looked forward to this and had a great time every time we went.

The Tape Recorder
A couple of weeks had passed since our Florida trip, and I was sitting in the living room one Saturday evening late doing some studying on a management course I was taking. I had all my stuff spread out on the dining room table and included in this stuff was a tape recorder. It was late about eleven thirty in the evening. The children and gone to bed and so had Sylvia. It was quiet. I heard a little boy come up behind me and say, "Daddy, what are you doing?" It was Michael. I explained to him what I was doing and he asked if he could sit with me a while. I said sure.

And we visited just a little bit, and he asked me what that machine was. I said it was a tape recorder, and he asked how it worked. I showed him and he asked if he could try it. I said sure. So he took the mic in his hand and asked me what he should say. I said how about talking about your Florida trip? He said that would be good, so he started. He went on to tell what a great time he had and all the things that we did. It was a pretty extensive story, and finally he got sleepy and said, "I gotta go to bed, Daddy. I'm too tired."

I took him back and said good night. I didn't realize at the time that tape would become so important in my life. I labeled it and put it up somewhere. I kept it for a long time and I lost it in Hurricane Katrina.

Michael and His Music
Michael always used to clown around like he was singing into a microphone, he would take a flat knife, turn it around and pretend the

handle was a microphone. He would start singing into it and dancing around having the best time. I think he liked to perform. He had two songs he was particularly fond of it that time, one was *Jennifer Tomkins*, and his all-time favorite was *Big Bad Leroy Brown*. He sang that song a lot.

The Children's Christmas Shopping

I encouraged the children to save their money so they could go Christmas shopping every year. And they did. We made a really big deal out of it. I took them to the mall and found a good place to sit down I'd have a cup of coffee or soft drink send them on their way. They would make a list out long in advance of the shopping trip and spread out into the mall to buy the gifts. This particular shopping spree, they would bring gifts back, lay them on the table next to me and say, "We're not through yet. We'll be back in a minute." But finally they were pretty much shopped out and they came back to the table and sat down.

I don't remember which one of them asked me, but the question soon came up. "Daddy, we need to borrow a little money from you. Will you make us a loan?" I asked what they wanted a loan for. They said they had found a wonderful pocketknife for Granddaddy but didn't have quite enough money left. So I gave them the money they wanted and they scampered back to the mall, and soon they were back with the pocketknife. They just enjoyed wrapping the presents and giving them away at Christmas time. It was a great relationship to develop with my children.

The Spanking

Early one evening we were headed home and had Catherine with us in the car, and she said I want to stop at the market to pick up a few things. I said okay and stopped. She got out of the car and headed towards the market. The boys said they wanted to go with her. I said, "Okay but don't you pester her and ask buy you anything or I'll give you a spanking when we get home." So I let them out and off to the store they went.

Catherine was walking around the market getting what she wanted, and I could see through the window that they were pulling on her dress talking to her. They all got back in the car, and I turned around to the back seat, and said, "Did you ask your grandma to buy you anything?" There was a long silence, and they admitted they had. I said, "Okay, when you get home I'm going to keep my word and give you spanking. Catherine was fit to be tied said I'd better not spank the children. I didn't answer.

We let her out at her house and continued home. I cut a little switch from the backyard and proceeded with my promise. I took their little britches down and switched the boys good across their butts. They cried a little bit, but it was soon over and they had a bath.

We had supper and I was reading to them sitting in my lounge chair with them sitting by my side when the doorbell rang. It was Catherine; she had walked all way up from her house and was all out of breath. She came into the house and asked if I had whipped boys. I said yes. She turned to the children and asked if I had hurt them. They said not too bad. She settled down and Sylvia finally drove her back to her house.

Baseball on Saturday Morning

We had an unusually large backyard and I would hit grounders and fly balls to the children in the neighborhood. This Saturday morning there were about six of them when we started. After a while it to got down to just Johnny and Mike. They were having a good time and I was whacking the balls pretty hard. One of the grounders took a bad hop and hit Johnny right in the nose. He started bleeding pretty bad so I got a handkerchief and got it to stop. We took a break and had a drink.

I said we should call it a day, but Johnny wanted to play some more. We continued on for pretty good while. But I learned one thing about my son John that particular moment: that he was not a quitter. He has proven that all of his life and am so proud of him for that.

Saturday Morning Hard Work

Our house was new and needed some work in the flowerbeds. So this Saturday morning Johnny, Mike, and I decided to plant some flowers. It was rather warm and got kinda hot, so I said, "Michael, why don't you go into the carport and get Daddy a beer, and you and Johnny a drink." He said okay and left.

We continued our yard work, but he didn't come back, and I got worried so I went looking for him. He was under the carport sipping one of my beers. I said, "Michael how does it taste?" He said, "It's pretty good, Daddy." I said, "Well, you give it to me and you get you a drink and one for Johnny and we will go back to work. He said okay. He could be a little devil sometimes.

The Serious Lesson

I came home one evening and Sylvia pulled me aside and said I needed to talk to Michael. I asked what about. She said evidently he had pulled little girl's pants down who lived across the street from us. Her mother was really upset and came over and told Sylvia that she needed to speak to her son. She told her she would but thought she would leave it up to me. I didn't know quite how to handle it, so I said I'd take it up with him in the morning.

Since Johnny was not involved in the situation I told Sylvia to take him shopping. I didn't really know quite how to handle that but I came up with a plan. I took him in the back bathroom stood him up on the toilet seat, where we would be about eye-level to me. I started shaving and talking to him but not looking at him directly. I asked if he had pulled the girl's pants down. He said yes. I lectured him and told him that was not a good thing to do and was terribly wrong and we didn't do those kinds of things.

Now Michael if you did not look him straight in the eye, he had a tendency to shape the truth little bit at times so I took ahold of his chin and looked him right in the eye and said, "Michael, you have to promise Daddy that you will never do that again."

He looked right at me and said, "Daddy, I promise you I will never do that again but I don't promise you I won't want to do it again." Before I answered, I thought a minute and then said, "Good enough."

Michael was always fond of little girls and we had to keep a close eye on him most of the time when they were around. On Saturday morning I was in the back bedroom and it was a warm day and all the windows were open and they were screened. I was sitting on the edge of the bed reading something, and I heard this voice right under my window. "Why don't you lay on the blanket with me right here." He was talking to some little girl and didn't know I was around, so I coughed very loud. I put an end to that episode.

Johnny's Big Bass

Some friends of mine had bought a house out in the country, and it had a large pond in front of it. I had asked them if I could bring my children out there sometime, and they said okay. Michael didn't much care for fishing so I just planned to take Johnny on the trip. We were talking to his granddaddy about going out there and fishing for bass. I didn't know a thing about fishing for bass so he got some good advice.

Granddaddy told him to get some large night crawlers, some good strong line, and some corks. He said, "When you get to the pond, you put a lot of big night crawlers on your hook. Then put the cork on the line about four feet from the hook. Throw it out in the middle as far as you can throw it and then just sit and wait. Keep a close eye on the cork and when it starts to bob up and down don't do a thing but wait." Granddaddy lit up a cigarette took a couple of puffs. He said, "When the cork goes under and starts to move around, pull back on your rod real hard and set the hook."

121

Johnny followed his directions and caught a fish, and boy it was a beauty. We didn't have a net so I told him to start walking back up the bank and keep the line tight and I would try to get something to get the bass out of the water. I found an old board close at hand and when the bass got up close enough to the shore I put the board under it and tried to flip it up on the ground. Johnny was still pulling the backward. It weighed almost eight pounds. He entered it in the contest that the local TV station had on the weekend and won second place.

There was another place Johnny and I fished way out in the country. It was back in the woods and nobody had probably fished there in years. We used to go out there and really catch bass. I had a plug called the Budweiser plug. It was shaped just like a Budweiser can only much smaller and came in two parts. It made a lot of racket when you pulled it through the water and the fish just could not leave it alone. It was so overgrown out there, one day it got caught up in the tree and I never could get it back. Johnny used to catch bass there all the time and he took his granddaddy out there with him several times. It was a good fishing pond.

Michael's Billy Tooker cap.

Michael had a brown stocking cap he called his Billy Tooker cap, and when the weather was cold he always wore it riding his bicycle. I would see him riding down the road in front of the house, he would throw up his hand and say, "Hey, Daddy." I still have this cap. Later on in my memoirs I will talk about this cap.

Moving to Gulfport, Mississippi

July 1971 I was promoted to the district manager the Gulfport, Mississippi, office. I had worked hard to get the promotion and had a very good teacher. I had learned a lot from my manager.

The children were excited about moving to Gulfport, as were Sylvia and I. We looked on the map to see where Gulfport was actually located, and knew we would be close to the ocean. The company was going to move us so we had to find a place to live temporarily. One of the agents who worked in my district had a house for rent so we rented it and moved in.

The weekend we moved into this house there was a deep sea fishing rodeo in Gulfport. We had never seen anything like that and the kids and I were really excited about going.

It was on a weekend, I believe Friday night, and Michael complained of having a headache. He never had any headaches had never been sick. He didn't complain too much so Saturday we started to unpack, and that evening Michael complained some more about his headache. That night he had a restless night and came into our bed in the middle of the night and asked if he could sleep with us.

On Sunday the rodeo was in full swing. So we headed down to the Gulfport beach. It was quite a sight to see for us because we had never seen anything like this with all those fish. We had a good time, though Michael didn't seem to feel too good, but we didn't think it was anything serious.

CHAPTER 12

Hard Times

Disaster Strikes

It was Monday and I had to go to the district office to meet all my employees and take over my job as manager. I left home about seven thirty and arrived at the office. At about nine thirty, Johnny called me and said I'd better get home because Michael was really sick. I couldn't imagine what was wrong with him. But I did hurry on home, and he was in bad shape.

Michael was having convulsions one right after another, and we had never ever seen anything like that. We loaded him in the car and headed for the hospital. I'd seen the sign on the road that showed way to the hospital. When we got there he was still convulsing and they took him right on into the emergency room and started treatment. The convulsions finally stopped and they put him in a private room to do some tests.

The wife of the agent we had rented the house from was a nurse and her name was Jean. She showed up in the hospital almost the same time we did. She suggested that she take Johnny to her house. Sylvia and I just sat around and waited for any kind of news about Michael.

He was sitting up in bed at suppertime and they bought him a tray, and I tried to feed him. He was not his usual self, and at one point he started to eat his napkin. I knew then that something was very, very wrong with Michael. The preliminary diagnosis was spinal meningitis, but that was not confirmed. He wasn't getting any better with the treatment, and finally lapsed into a coma. They had no idea what was wrong with Michael or how to treat him.

The doctor suggested we get a specialist from Ochsner Clinic in New Orleans. The next day he came in and examined Michael. Sylvia and I were anxiously sitting outside his room waiting for the report and it was not good. The doctor said that Michael had no response to any stimuli whatsoever. His examination showed no brain function at all. He was on full life-support and retaining fluid in his lungs which they had to pump out constantly. He wasn't getting any better and it appeared he was getting a lot worse.

At the beginning of the third week, Sylvia and I had had to make a decision. We had tried everything, playing music, reading to him and all that stuff, and nothing seemed to work. So we decided to go talk to the local priests. We told them of the situation and asked what to do. We discussed taking him off life support completely, and the priest agreed that that might be the best option. On the way back to the hospital, Sylvia and I decided that's what we would do.

We arrived at the hospital and I told Sylvia to wait outside the room while I talked to the nurse. I told her to unplug everything and close the door and leave me alone with him. She did. Looking at him, I just couldn't believe what had happened. He had lost so much weight. His little hands were so thin, and he just didn't look like Michael.

When he was younger I had given him two silver dollars with his birth date on them. I had them in my pocket and I placed one in each side of his pajama pockets and laid my head down on his heart. It was barely beating. I listened to it for just a short while until I could no longer hear it. I said, "Sweet dreams, I love you, Michael. I just cried and cried and cried. I just couldn't believe he was gone. And as I write this horrible incident I still cry. No one ever gets over the death of a child.

The Funeral

My promotion had turned into a disaster. We were in a strange place with no friends and nobody to turn to. Johnny, Sylvia and I were just totally devastated. I had made arrangements for the funeral to be held at St. Patrick's Church in Phenix City, Alabama. He is buried at the Lakeview Cemetery there. His marker has a quote, "Sweet dreams, I love you."

Father Conroy at St. Patrick's Church did the service. In his remarks he made the statement, "I'm called to do a lot of funerals for people I did not know and never met. This is not the case with Michael; he served as an altar boy with his brother Johnny and I knew both of them well. Michael was a good boy and I will always remember him for that." All our friends were at the funeral. My mother and brother Bruce had come down from Vermont to attend the funeral.

Back to Gulfport

Johnny was enrolled at St. Thomas school and I was trying to work. Sylvia was devastated and was not coping very well at all. She had become a total recluse. Not getting dressed, not going to the store, not eating, and I was really worried. Johnny had gone out for football, and obviously this was good for him. He took all his frustrations and anger out on the football field and it helped him a lot.

I came home one day, and Johnny was sitting in the bed with big tears running down his face. I said, "What is the matter, son?" He said, "I don't know, Daddy." I was really worried about him too. The saying is time stands still for no man. So we just floundered around day by day.

Michael when he was younger in the cooler weather wore a stocking cap. It was brown. When he was riding his bike he would throw up his arm and say, "Hey, Daddy." I kept this hat. I took it to my office and kept it in my drawer. Several times a week, I would close the door, take out this hat and just sniff it. I could smell the presence of his body and have a good cry.

Every weekend for a long period of time we would head back to Phenix City. I really don't know why; it just seemed the right thing to do.

Panic Attack

Johnny was in a play at St. Thomas church for a school function. He had a part in the play where he was doing the soft shuffle dance. He had practiced really hard and was pretty good at it. He was anxious for me and his mama to see him in the play.

We had a problem with the time because we had gone to a convention in West Palm Beach, Florida, and were cutting it really close to get back for that Friday evening play. The convention was to end on Friday morning, so we decided to check out real early about two a.m. We started for Gulfport, Mississippi, and were going to drive all day to get there in time for the play I had a new Buick and hoped we would not have any car trouble. I had driven from West Palm Beach to Bainbridge, Georgia.

The strangest thing happened to me that morning, and never has happened again. I must've had a panic attack or something. I just got so nervous I had to stop and Sylvia had started driving. I was in a terrible state. She had some pills that she took to calm her down so I took one of them. I crawled into the backseat, fell sound asleep, and Sylvia drove the rest of the way by herself. It's a long way from Bainbridge, Georgia, to Gulfport, Mississippi.

We got there in time to watch the play and to see Johnny do his part. He was very good at it and I'm glad we made the trip but we were both exhausted.

Scary Discovery

People would sometimes transfer their insurance from Alabama to all parts of the country. Our job was to locate the new address they had given to set them up for service.

I and my sales manager were working on a transfer way out in the country in Bay St. Louis, Mississippi. We had some directions on how to reach this place but it was really isolated. We got some last minute instructions from a little small country store in that area. We drove a few more miles to the end of the road.

There was an old house where somebody was living. There was a large barn with several stalls for horses. No one was about, and we knocked on the door. No answer. So we moseyed on down to the barn and hollered, "Anybody here?" No answer so we entered the barn which was open and I took one side and my sales manager took the other side and we walked into the barn.

About halfway down my sales manager said, "Come here and look at this. Up against the wall in one of the stalls was a machine gun. When we saw it we made a beeline for the car and got the hell out of there as fast as we could. We had stumbled upon probably some illegal activity and didn't want to get shot.

We left word for the account holders at the country store about what we were doing at the house so that if they came by the store he would tell them what was going on. They called us a couple of days later and came by the office and we got the issue straightened out.

Gunpoint

One morning in the district office, this man came in very, very irritated. He had his son with him and was upset about a claim his daughter had with the company. She had had a stillbirth, and the policy stated the amount of money it would pay for the claim. He was not satisfied at all, and said the agent had told his daughter differently. The girls at the front desk could not calm him down. He began to get more and more agitated. He finally pulled out a gun and threatened to shoot the agent.

I had my door closed but I could hear some of the conversation and I opened the door. He turned around and pointed the gun at me. He said, "Who are you?" I told him I was a district manager and if he would come into my office, I would try to settle his complaint. He came into the office with his son and I closed the door. He put the gun down by his side and I listened to his story.

The company had always been there for any policyholder who felt mistreated. I knew I had some negotiating room and I used it. I said, "What did the agent tell your daughter?" He stated the amount the agent had told him the company would pay. I think it was $500 more than the policy called for. I assured him we would pay the $500 and said I was sorry about that and asked him if that would be okay. He said that would be just fine. So he left, and none of us were shot at that scary moment.

Office Fire

I was having considerable trouble with an agent who was very dishonest and had broken all the company rules. I had documentation to show him every case and I had to fire him. I did not realize at the time that what was going to happen would have a big impact on our office for several weeks.

Somehow during the night, he got into the office looking for the documents that I had used to fire him with. He could not find them as I had taken them with me to the house. He then proceeded to set fire to the district office. Fortunately the fire was put out fairly early but the office was full of smoke and it was hard to breathe in there. We had to call a specialist in to remove the odor, redo the ceiling fiberglass, and pump air into the sealed building. It was a terrible mess that caused a lot of problems for us for several weeks. But we managed and somehow got right back on track. I never could prove that the agent started the fire but there was no other person I knew of who had any reason to seek revenge.

CHAPTER 13

Starting to Heal

Decision About My Job

We were still having a lot of trouble adjusting to the loss of Michael, and Sylvia and I had discussed several options. None were very good. So I sought the advice of one of my vice presidents in the home office. We made an appointment, took Johnny to Phenix City, left him with his grandmother, and headed towards Birmingham, Alabama.

We had a long meeting and talked about several things. I was assured that they would move me as soon as possible if that's what I wished. They also told me that moving was not going to change the hurt that we felt. So we left and headed back to Phenix City to pick up Johnny.

On the way we talked a lot about what we should do and what we shouldn't do and we came to conclusion that we would just go back and tough it out. Sylvia suggested that we have a party for all employees at the house. I was kinda shocked at this but I thought that was a good idea and would help her. She took care of everything and the party was a huge success and it really helped her.

Sorority Sisters

Our friend Jean Russell belonged to a sorority and she had a friend named Al Leonard. She was a retired registered nurse and would come to the house with Jean to visit with Sylvia. It just so happened that she was married and lived in Ludlow, Vermont, which was where I was born and raised. So we hit it off right away. Al was involved in helping young boys who were medically and physically having a very difficult time. She used to visit them at their homes and do what she could for them. She invited Sylvia to go on one of these visits with her.

This particular young boy was in a full body cast. Sylvia told me that was the most pitiful sight. She felt so sorry for that little fella, and she made several visits with Al to his house. This seemed to bring Sylvia out more and more, and that was a good thing. I was working very hard, and Johnny was doing good in school and in football.

Our First Fishing Trip in the Ocean

We only lived a short walk from the oceanfront, and Johnny wanted to go fishing. I said okay and went to buy some fish poles and shrimp. I also bought a small rubber raft which was cheap as dirt but it served the purpose temporarily. We walked down to the beach, put our stuff in the little boat, and paddled out to the furthest piling we could see. We tied the rubber raft up through a line in the water.

We'd only been there a short time when Johnny looked out and said that the water was turning black. It was a fairly large mass, and it was kind of bubbling on the water. I told him we'd better head back for sure because I didn't know what that was. So we untied little rubber raft and started paddling back. We kept looking over our shoulder to see what was going on, and spotted some large fins in the water.

Oh my goodness, I thought, those are sharks. So we paddled very hard to get to the beach. We didn't hang around there very long and went back to the house. We found out later what this was. It was a school of mullet and chasing them were porpoises. The common phrase around Biloxi, Mississippi, for this type of activity is called "smoking the water." Mullet are also called Biloxi bacon. So we found out what all that was about.

Johnny's Eye Surgery at Johns Hopkins in Baltimore, Maryland
Our next-door neighbor was a nurse who worked for an optometrist. The optometrist had just come back from a convention somewhere out of the country and our neighbor was telling him about Johnny's problem with his eyelids. He had a condition called bilateral ptosis, which means his eyelids drooped, giving him a sleepy look and making it hard for him to open his eyes wide. Evidently this was something that had been discussed at this convention. He told our neighbor the name of the doctor at Johns Hopkins and said he would write a letter or make an appointment with him.

We had nothing to lose and everything to gain so we made the appointment. We went to his office where he examined Johnny thoroughly. This type of surgery was his specialty and he was probably, if not the best, one of the best, in the country. After examining Johnny he turned to the boy and asked, "Are you ready for me to do the job?"

Johnny looked surprised. He turned to me and his mama and asked what we thought. I looked at the doctor and asked, "Can you fix the problem?" He said, "I certainly can." So I said, "Let's do it."

Johnny had the surgery and he had to spend the night in the hospital. The nurses told Sylvia to stay in the room and not leave without having someone with her. They said it might be too dangerous because the hospital was in a very bad neighborhood. The next day the doctor came in and examined Johnny. He took the bandages off and said, "Son, look in the mirror now and tell me what you think." The doctor told us everything was fine and we could go back to the hotel that night. He said there was no need for us to come back to the hospital the next day, but that he would meet us at a different location. He gave us directions told us what time.

While Johnny was looking in the mirror, he told Sylvia to call his grandma. She did and when he got on the phone, he said, "Oh, Grandma, I'm so beautiful now. We knew then that this had bothered Johnny a lot more than we realized. We were discharged and went back to the hotel and made an appointment the next day at the location the doctor had told us about. He examined Johnny and said everything looked fine, gave us some prescriptions.

We checked out and headed back home. The surgery was a great success, and to my knowledge Johnny's never had any serious problem with his eyelids again. Maybe occasional dry eyes but that's all. Thanks to our neighbor.

Basketball in the Driveway

Johnny loved basketball, and so did I. We used to play one on one in the driveway a lot of times. One Saturday night we were out there pretty late, having a good time. I'd say it was about ten thirty. A police car drove up in the driveway, and a policeman got out. He said he'd had a complaint about us making too much noise this late at night. He chuckled to himself and told us to just tone it down a little bit. He said, "My job would be a whole lot easier if this was the only type of complaint I got." We continued playing until both of us were tired out. I really enjoyed these outings and I think Johnny did to.

Our First Hurricane

This hurricane was projected to hit the coast. So we loaded up the car and headed to the office. It was in a much better location away from the water. We monitored the storm's progress that evening, and the report said it had turned and was not going to hit our area. We would only get some minor wind. So we loaded the car back up and headed back to the house. It was probably midnight or later when we drove back up Highway 90. Everything was desolate, no cars, all the houses boarded up; it was kinda spooky. There was a big tree off to the right side of the driveway and when we got home, I swung wide enough to put my headlights on it to see if there was any damage. There was none so I backed into the driveway. My headlights did not shine on the house as they would normally.

I got out of the car started up the walkway to the front door. I heard voices inside the house. I knew then that somebody was trying to rob us. I turned back towards the car and I told Johnny to hand me the shotgun out of the trunk. He did and as I approached the front door I heard the night latch click. I knew then the only way out was through the back, so I ran around by the back door and when I got to the patio I saw this young man almost to the top of the fence. I shouted at him, "You'd better stop or I'll shoot you."

He had just reached the top and tumbled over onto the ground and ran into the woods. I sure am glad I didn't have to shoot him because he was young boy. The other guy had jumped out the bathroom window and I never did get to see him. They had piled everything they wanted to take into the front room and were waiting for their truck to load it onto. They didn't get much, just a few coins, but several of my neighbors had got cleaned out. Looting is a major problem when hurricanes occur.

Sharon
Johnny was in school, doing well in sports, and working hard. He met this young lady named Sharon. He dated her all through high school and they got married while he was in college. Sharon was a wonderful girl, a good wife, and a good mother. She and Johnny worked very hard all their lives.

Unfortunately Sharon at age fifty-five suddenly dropped dead at work. This could have been the ruination of Johnny. They were so much in love and had worked so hard to achieve what they had done. Losing his brother Michael was so hard for him, and now losing Sharon. This was going to be a very, very hard time for Johnny. He had just gotten promoted to CEO of his company, and they had made fabulous plans for their future. Bought a big brand-new home and everything seemed to be going just right.

There is nothing I could say or do to help the situation except to be there if he needed me. But the good Lord took charge. Johnny began to slowly realize life his was never going to be the same. Johnny had always been an achiever, and as I related earlier he was not a quitter, and he didn't quit. I'm so grateful that he had this trait because it helped him adjust.

Cindy

One evening on his way home, Johnny spotted this dog by the Boy Scout hut. The dog had evidently broken loose from somewhere. She had a cord around her neck and was going through the garbage. Johnny brought her home and cared for her. We advertised and watched everything to see if somebody would claim her. No one ever did and we named her Cindy. She was the best bird-dog I had ever seen. She came by it naturally and was never trained.

Johnny had a friend named Ricky whose daddy had a farm in the country. They used to like to go up there to hunt. Johnny asked me if he could take Cindy to do some bird hunting. I said, "Sure but do not shoot any birds over her until she learns to point and hold it." He said okay so I guess he spent about a week up there deer hunting and letting Cindy chase birds. Johnny said she used to find them and chase them. After a while she realized she couldn't catch them so she just starting pointing and holding. That was the making of a great bird-dog with absolutely no training.

When I took her bird hunting she could always find birds if they were around. Sometimes quail would run to ground from the point of contact. When the birds would run she would still stay on point but the tip of her tail would quiver. I had noticed this several times. So one time when this it happened, I said, "Okay, Cindy, find them. She broke point and located them again. She was such a great bird-dog.

— PART 5 —

CONVENTIONS, TRAVEL, AND FUN

CHAPTER 14

Liberty National Perks

The wonderful conventions we had at Liberty National were earned. They got better as the years went on and there were many but I would like to talk about four of them. There was a Hawaii convention, a Breakers convention in West Palm Beach, a Paris convention, and a Rome convention.

The very first convention I went to was in Biloxi, Mississippi, at the Broadwater Beach Hotel. At that time it was the finest place on the coast. It was a wonderful spot, and I was impressed with the president of the company. When we were unloading in the front of the hotel the president was standing there greeting all of us. He called me by my first name and called my wife by her first name. I thought this was pretty impressive for him to take the time to learn all the first names of all the participants.

The seafood was great, the golf was great and we had a great time.

Paris Convention

The Paris convention was one of the best I had ever been to and there were so many sites to see, historical and otherwise, and lots of entertainment. We had plenty of free time to shop during the day and had several tours, one of which was the Palace of Versailles, which as you know was an historic site.

The funniest thing happened to me while I was at the palace. I had picked up the bad habit of chewing tobacco a couple years before and was looking for a place to hide somewhere and have a chew. I found a little corner, got out my package of Red Man, and began to have a good chew. I had been there just a few minutes when I looked around and there was one of my fellow employees from Andalusia, Alabama, and he was looking for a place to chew also. It was cold and damp and we didn't stay there too long but we had a good visit and enjoyed our chew.

We saw some great shows in the evenings at several clubs. Sylvia wanted to go to the Louvre and she went with some of the ladies. One day we were walking down the street, and this raggedy looking homeless man jumped out of an alley and held a rat right in front of Sylvia's face. I don't know why he did, but it scared the daylights out of us. He disappeared as quickly as he appeared. And we went on our way a lot more cautiously.

France is noted for its wonderful perfumes, one of them being Joy by Jean Patou. It had the most wonderful aroma and I thought Sylvia would like it, so I bought a bottle. I continued doing this on our anniversary every year until she passed away after nearly sixty years of marriage. I had purchased a bottle just before she died and I still have it. I have no idea what I'll do with it but I'm going to keep it.

One of the evenings the company had planned for us was an eight-course dinner atop the Eiffel Tower. Of course we had seen this historical site in movies and magazines. But to be able to ride the elevator to the very top and have this wonderful meal was special. The food was terrific, the wine was terrific, and the music was terrific. After we finished eating, which took a long time, the large tables were cleared to make room for a dance floor. Then the orchestra came out and played for a long time. We danced and drank a lot of wine. This was a fabulous night for all of us. There were so many other things that we did I'm sure I'll leave some of them out but it was a fabulous convention.

West Palm Beach Convention

This was as swanky a place as I had ever seen. It was for the ultra-rich for many years and part of the Flagler estate, which was extremely private and not open to the public. Over the years to raise money, the Breakers opened it up to conventions for large companies. It had several golf courses, tennis courts, and swimming pools. For dinner you had to wear a coat and tie in the dining room, which was filled with wonderful paintings.

All the big-name celebrities had stayed there at one time or another and when we were there a singer named Engelbert Humperdinck was staying there. He was not performing, just vacationing.

Sylvia and I had the most fabulous room I've ever stayed in overlooking the beach with a large veranda, and a huge bedroom and living area. It was the most romantic setting we had ever experienced. In the evening when we sat out on the veranda, the lights would come on under the water as far as we could see. If the moon was up, and the lights were on, the ocean was simply beautiful. Sylvia and I talked about that a long time after we made the convention.

Hawaii Convention

We had qualified for the convention to Hawaii so Sylvia's mother and daddy came and stayed with Johnny in Long Beach. We had a wonderful time and saw everything. Hawaii is such a beautiful place. One of the things of interest was the hang gliders over the cliffs. The wind would draft up against the high walls of the cliff and enable the hang gliders to stay up there as long as they wished.

We had a tour and looked into the side of the mountains where there were caves. History tells us that people of wealth would keep their possessions in these caves about halfway down the mountain. They would lower slaves to store their possessions, and when the slaves completed their tasks, the owners would cut the ropes and the slaves would drop in the ocean and drown.

The palm trees along the main road in downtown had big, wide metal bands all around them. I was curious enough to ask questions about them. I was told that several years ago the islands were full of snakes. In order to get rid of the snakes, they brought in the mongoose. All that accomplished what they set out to do, but without snakes the rats began to multiply. These metal bands around the palm trees were to keep the rats from climbing up the trees and jumping into buildings downtown. I'm assuming now that there are a lot of mongoose. My neighbor just got back from there and said they were everywhere. There were so many other things but I don't have time to elaborate on all them.

Rome Convention
We took a two-week vacation prior to the convention in Rome. One week on our own, and the other week at the convention. Two other couples with us decided to take a tour. We rented a van in Rome. When we landed, we loaded our luggage and everything in the van and took off. We had no planned itinerary but a general idea of where we would like to go.

We started out heading for Germany. Our plan was to tour Germany, go over the Alps and down the Italian side and end up in Rome. It was wintertime, snowing a lot and cold. When we reached the base of the Alps, we had to take a train through the tunnel to get to the other side headed towards Zürich. You had to drive your car up onto a railroad car, and they would drive through the tunnel to get you on the other side. This was a most unusual thing we had seen.

We arrived on the other side and headed down the mountains to get to the city of Zürich. Zürich is a wealthy city with a lot of fabulous stores. We had only heard of Zürich in the movies and magazines and were eager to take it all in.

The first thing I noticed was that all the ladies were really dressed up. I would have to note that they were not the prettiest women in the world, not like down south but they were all dressed really nice.

We walked around and looked in all the shops. We found a place that sold exclusive watches. It was four stories high, and very expensive. We didn't intend on buying anything there but we wanted to go inside so we all piled in the store. While we were there a lady came in wearing a turban, and a couple of large gentlemen were with her. She had taken the elevator up to the third floor where some expensive watches and jewelry were.

Sylvia and I decided to take the elevator up to see what she was doing. She immediately got attention of the clerk, and was shown the most expensive stuff in the store. She purchased several items. I did not see her pay for anything, but I noticed she had signed some kind of sales slip. She then left, and the two gentlemen left with her.

After seeing Zürich we decided to move on to our next destination. That would be Munich, Germany. We arrived late in the afternoon and had extreme difficulty finding a place to stay. There was some kind of Fasching fest going on at this time. There were no rooms available, and we really had to scurry around to find a place to sleep.

There was an old army barracks, which had these wooden bunks and in a two-story building. The bunks were too short for me, but it was a place to sleep. One of the unusual accommodations was the one large toilet at the end of the hallway. It had no doors and no stalls. There was an open shower with six showerheads in it but no privacy. It didn't seem to matter to anybody there; they just went on about their business. So we had to do the same if we wanted to take a shower or go to the bathroom and we survived.

We got up the next morning and spent some time in Munich and decided to go to the Black Forest which is on the way to the infamous Dachau prison camp. The Black Forest was extremely dark; there was a lot of growth and very little sunlight. When we emerged from the forest into the countryside, it was simply beautiful. There was green grass everywhere and a lot of pheasants. It truly was quite a sight.

We arrived at the prison camp. I had heard so much about this place, I was not comfortable at all. This is where the ovens were located where they cremated Jewish people and starved them to death. We took one quick tour on the inside, and Sylvia and I left and went back to the van. The other couples stayed a little longer and soon we were on our way again.

We kept on driving till evening and then found a place to stay. It was a nice bed and breakfast place very clean and very hospitable. It was near a fjord, where there were boats galore. We woke up the next morning, had a continental breakfast, and walked out the docks. We could see these large fish swimming around the docks and nobody fishing. I guess they weren't the right kind.

We then headed toward the Alps where we would cross over into Italy. We came to a little town called Mittenwald. We checked into this really nice little hotel that was like a chalet. They were very nice to us and we had some really nice rooms. It had snowed very hard and was very cold so we took time to unpack and relax. The rooms were small but nice and had radiators to keep you warm at night. We had a snack and all went to bed.

The next day we would start over the mountains as soon as possible. We loaded up the van and started toward the base of the mountain, only to find out that they were closing the road because it was impassable at the time. So we had to go back to the hotel and spend another night.

Sylvia and I decided to walk around the town and look at all the sights. This little town looked like a Christmas postcard, with quaint little shops and a beautiful church. We spent most of the afternoon walking around and looking.

When we got back to the hotel I asked the clerk if there was a good place to have supper. She told me there was a nice restaurant where the local people all went in the food was really good. She said they might be having some kind of party that night and we would have a good time if we went. So we decided to go eat there.

Boy was it great. The people were so nice to us, and we asked the waiter what he would recommend for supper. He recommended that we try the Yeager steak and a nice bottle of wine. So we did, and it was delicious. They had a dance floor and there was singing dancing and drinking a lot of wine. So we stayed there most of the evening and had a great time.

As we were leaving, the owner came over and gave us a really nice bottle of wine and said he thought we'd enjoy it. The other couples did not drink so we took the bottle back to the hotel and I set it out on the deck on the rail to keep it cool. The next morning when I woke up I could only see the very top it had snowed so hard. But no harm I just packed it in my suitcase and took it with me.

While Sylvia and I were shopping that afternoon, the other two couples had gone and purchased some chains so we could get over the mountain. Early that morning they had lifted the barriers so the mountain was open for traffic. We started up over the Alps and I'm telling you they are monstrous. I grew up in New England where we had some mountains but they would look like little bumps compared to the Alps. We traveled the really tiny little roads, with just room enough for two cars, and no room for error. Our driver had eased off to the side, and we got stuck. We had no idea how to get out.

There were a lot of young skiers traveling on the road that day. They stopped, helped us out and wished us well. They couldn't speak very good English but would not take anything for helping us. We were thankful that they were there. We started our descent from the Alps which took most all day.

As we left the higher elevation, the snow began to dissipate and green foliage was all around us. When we got to the Italian side, we stopped on the top to enjoy the view. We took some pictures and took it all in. As we began the descent towards the Adriatic Sea, the mountainside was covered with brooks and a lot of men were fly fishing. It was quite a sight to see.

We finally reached the Adriatic Sea, found a hotel, and checked in. Now the custom is when you check into a hotel over there, your passport is taken that night and returned to you the next morning. I was told I should not ever give up my passport because I'd probably never get home again. So we had a confrontation with the clerk and finally he agreed that we could keep our passports.

The room was nice, and the bathroom was clean. We found us a really nice place to eat. It was a club with a restaurant on one side and a bar and a dance floor on the other. We had a good meal and enjoyed ourselves. There were a lot of young people there partying and having a good time too.

After we finished our meal the owner came over to us and said he thought we'd better leave now. We couldn't understand why, and he said, "The folks here think you are all Russian and I don't want any trouble," so we left and went back to the hotel to spend the night.

When we arrived in Rome we were assigned gorgeous rooms and were looking forward to a wonderful week. The company was required to have business meetings for tax purposes but most of the time we were free to do whatever we wished to do.

We had a couple of scheduled tours. The most interesting one was the Basilica. Having read all about Michelangelo's paintings and how pristine the basement was for the paintings, we were looking forward to going down there.

It's hard to imagine how talented Michelangelo was. When you look up at the Sistine Chapel, you see these beautiful paintings and wonder how in the world could he paint those while lying on his back so close to the ceiling and do the curvature to make them come out right. They were just beautiful. There was no talking allowed and it was an extremely spiritual setting. We stayed there as long as we could and then left to go to the courtyard.

We then had another tour inside the Basilica to a huge church where history tells us that all the popes were buried underneath this church. Upon entering the church there was a beautiful sculpture called *Pieta*, which is a statue of Jesus. There was a large crowd and you had to walk in line past *Pieta* and you could touch it and make the sign of the cross. They were so many people in line that I could not get close enough to touch it with my right hand, so I touched it with my left hand, made the sign of the cross and went on with the tour. The tour was fairly lengthy but it was very interesting.

When we returned to the courtyard, I noticed my left hand was beginning to swell up. I had never had any problems with that before or since. This particular day it was very scary. I could not get my wedding ring off because my fingers were so swollen. In the meantime the pope came out on his balcony and blessed the crowd. And we left. Outside the Basilica my hand began to go back to normal. I never understood what caused it and it never happened again.

The things we saw that day were simply marvelous works of art. Everywhere we went we saw this historical city in all its splendor and history. The next day we were scheduled to go to Florence, which was a great tour. We went in the oldest church in the city. The tour guide told us that eight or nine generations of families had worked on this church. It was marvelous. He explained to us that there was one stone somewhere in the church that if removed, the church would crumble. It was just amazing to see all these things. The crowds that were touring were fairly large and you couldn't move too much.

When we got outside the church, Sylvia said, "Did you know someone tried to pick your pocket?" I said, "Oh you can't be serious." She said she saw him run his fingers all over my back pockets looking for my wallet. I had put my wallet in my front pocket after receiving advice about the chances of being pickpocketed. I always kept my hand on it wherever we were in a crowd and I didn't have any further trouble.

While we were in Florence I think I saw the most beautiful statue of Moses that I had ever seen. It was inside a church lighted so you could see all the features on his huge statue. As I sat there looking at the statue, I had the feeling that I could just walk up and say something to Moses, it was so realistic and so beautiful. The statue is close to eight feet tall and you could see the features in the muscles and the sandals and the laces on his legs, his beard, everything was just unreal.

Our next stop on the tour was the Coliseum and this has a

tremendous amount history. Parts of it were bombed out during WWII and it had never been restored. But as we toured around the Coliseum you could imagine where the gladiators stayed and where they fought in the arena and where the crowds cheered and watched the sports.

We toured some leather factories and there are several, and the merchandise was very inexpensive compared to the USA, probably due to taxes. Sylvia bought a couple of jackets, and I bought some cameo rings at the cameo factory.

Our next stop on the tour that evening was at this huge opera house. You don't see any of these in the USA but this thing was monstrous and had a large stage and a balcony all the way around it with tables and chairs so you could eat while the show was going on. While we were watching the show, something fell from above and landed on Sylvia's plate. It was a spoon that had toppled from somebody's dinner on the balcony above. There was no harm but could have been if it had hit Sylvia.

One of the opera singers had seen what had happened, and when the performance was over she graciously came up to Sylvia and presented her with a beautiful red rose. I have a good picture that. We saw so many things in Rome I can't begin to tell you all about. The trip was wonderful and our tour was outstanding and we were ready to get back to the USA.

Liberty National's Friday Meetings

When I was a sales manager in Columbus, Georgia, we used to have some really interesting Friday meetings. After taking care of business we always had a lot of fun. We had a young man named Elmer Snyder, and he was appointed the judge. He would take a large garbage bag, poke a hole in it and put it over his head like a robe and hold court. Some of this stuff was really ridiculous but very funny.

We also had planned fishing trips after Labor Day to Panama City, Florida. As an incentive we would pay for some of the trip or all of the trip if certain requirements were met. Everyone wanted to go. We checked in on Friday and got ready for a long early fishing trip Saturday morning. That Friday night we would all go out in different directions and have a good time.

One of our sales managers got a little bit sick during the night. He vomited several times and had a hard time. We were to leave on a fishing trip at five a.m., which was before daylight. He was my roommate, and when we got up that morning to leave for the fishing trip, he couldn't find his dentures. Lord, he was frantic so we started looking all over the floor, all over the place in the hotel room and could not locate them. The only conclusion was he may have lost them in the toilet during the night when he was sick. So we notified the hotel clerk of the incident and headed towards our all day fishing trip.

My friend was very uncomfortable all day long and could hardly wait to get back to the hotel to find out if they had located the dentures. When we got back to the hotel the commode was sitting out in front of the room. They had found his teeth and they were putting everything back together again. He was so relieved, as were all of us.

For several weeks after we returned to our office and regular work, on Fridays there would be a lot of jokes about this incident. It took a long time for this to go away.

Elmer and the Judge

Elmer was a real comedian and was always telling jokes. He told one story about a parking ticket he had received and went to a judge to try to get it torn up. The judge was on his way somewhere in the hallway and Elmer kept after him about tearing up the ticket. The judge said, "I won't do it, Elmer." Well the judge was on his way to the restroom and he told Elmer, "I've got to go in here." Elmer said, "Judge, I surely don't have to go but I think I'll go pull out with you." The judge broke out into laughter and tore the ticket up. I thought this was hilarious.

Employee trip to Panama City Florida
Soon after Labor Day, I would take some of our employees to Panama City, Florida, for a long weekend. We would make some kind of incentive to help them pay for the trip so everyone could probably come. This particular time we had checked in early in the evening on Friday and went out the have a few drinks. The next morning some of the guys went fishing, and some of us went out to the swimming pool.

There wasn't anybody else at the pool but our employees and we were having a good time. One of my agents had a glass eye, due to an injury when he was a child. He usually wore a black patch over his eye, but for some reason had taken the patch off and was swimming around in the pool, and none of us were paying much attention because we were used to seeing him.

When he jumped up on the diving board and dove in the water, the pressure from the dive popped his glass eye out and it was somewhere in the pool. When he came up he started hollering, "Oh, my glass eye!" It was small enough to where it would roll towards the drain in the center of the pool, and we had to retrieve it before it disappeared forever. So we all started diving down and searching the bottom of the pool. Finally someone came up with it, and said, "I got it I got it."

This was very unusual and we laughed about it afterwards. This agent would make a joke of it later on, and say to us, "You all go ahead and I'll keep an eye out for you."

Mardi Gras
All along the coastal areas from Mobile to New Orleans, Mardi Gras was a big deal. Since we hadn't grown up in the area, this was all new to us. Employees had one week's vacation during Mardi Gras at most places, and this was standard. They had big parades leading up to the crowning of the Queen and King of Mardi Gras, lots of parties, raising money and just having a good time.

Sylvia belonged to a sorority that sponsored a big float in one of the parades. She was crowned queen of the sorority that year and rode on the float. The sorority had several parties and most of the people who belonged to the sorority were a lot older and had no connection with the insurance industry whatsoever. We used to really enjoy ourselves and made a lot of good friends.

CHAPTER 15

Wiggins, Mississippi

We were all working hard and doing fine, and I acquired a bird dog named Buck. Soon we had a litter of puppies and they were really pretty little dogs. Cindy was the mama and Buck was the dad. I used to come home in the afternoons and fool around with these bird dogs on a regular basis. I spent more and more time with them, and my involvement was getting to be too much.

I came home one day and I told Sylvia maybe I'd like to move to the country. This turned out not to be a good move for me and Sylvia, but since it was just the two of us, she loved me enough and said okay. We started looking for a place to move. Each weekend we would ride out in the countryside and try to find us a nice location.

We found a nice place in Wiggins, Mississippi, which was about twenty-five miles from the coast. It was far enough to be out of direct hit from a hurricane on the water, and it would give me time to fool with these dogs.

New Home

After we sold our house in Long Beach and moved to Wiggins, I would drive to work every morning, and drive home every night. I would leave early on Friday to spend the weekend at our new home. I built some very expensive dog kennels. Sylvia and I worked hard cleaning off the land, sling-blading and burning brush. I do believe that she and I had the most peaceful time while living in Wiggins getting our land and house in order.

We had a neighbor who was a retired heavy equipment operator and had a large bulldozer. He came down and helped us clean the rest of the land, and we worked really hard cleaning the place up. Sylvia decided she would have a nice garden, something we had never had before, but our neighbor Bill helped clear the land and plow the rows, and Sylvia had a nice garden of about thirty rows.

Yellow Jackets

On Saturday morning we were out working in the yard sling-blading away, and Sylvia evidently hit a spot that had a yellow jacket nest underneath it. They came after her in a big way. I got her in the house, we got her jeans off, and she had several bites on her legs. It was on a weekend and there was no emergency room close by. I knew these things could be very dangerous.

I had a friend who was a veterinarian who lived in Wiggins, and he was the only medical person I could think of right away. I called him and told him what happened. He said get a big chunk of Red Man chewing tobacco, get it good and wet, and make a poultice. Put it on each one of those sting bites and have Sylvia lie down and rest. So we proceeded to cover her legs with tobacco and hope there were no problems.

Sylvia never ran a fever so you couldn't tell if she had a severe infection. She rested the rest of the day and the night. She was in some pain but finally fell asleep. The next morning I took the poultice off. The swelling had gone down and she apparently was going to be okay. It's a good thing I chewed tobacco back then.

Ricky's Deer

One evening, about eleven o'clock when we were living in Wiggins, I had a knock on my door. It was Johnny's friend Ricky. He asked me if he could use the backyard to dress out a deer that had been hit by a car. I said sure. So they pulled around in the backyard and proceeded with their business.

I decided to have a little fun, and I got dressed went around the front of the house with my big flashlight and surprised them with the light, and said, "What the hell are y'all doing out here?" They did not know who it was and I'm sure they thought it was a game warden. I laughed and I said, "No worry, Ricky, it's just me."

They proceeded with their business and cleaned up real good. About three weeks later Ricky came by and left me several packages of frozen deer meat and it was really pretty good.

Field Trials

I had joined the South Mississippi Bird Hunters Association and entered my dogs and some field trials. Sylvia would go with me and make the best of it. We had a field trial somewhere near Hattiesburg, Mississippi, one weekend. I had entered Buck, and Johnny had entered his little puppy Belle. At the field trials they put domestic birds out, which do not have the ability to fly as quickly as wild birds. It was kind of damp that morning, and the birds they put out had spent the night in an open cage.

They send you out in what's called a brace with another bird dog. Buck had a terrific nose. He found the first seven birds, chased them all and caught them. This is a no-no for a bird dog. It took a long time to break him from doing that. In little while the puppy stakes were coming up and Belle was off and running. I heard an awful lot of shooting out there and when he finished I asked Johnny how he had done. He said okay.

It was getting late in the afternoon and I said maybe we'd better start home. He wanted to wait to see who had won. I knew it wasn't me, so it had to be him. Sure enough he had won first place in the puppy stakes with Belle. He got a nice trophy and a lot of praise for his dog. That little dog would do anything Johnny asked him to do.

Hurricane

This hurricane came up the Alabama-Mississippi line; it was actually the first hurricane we had experienced close by. That night it sounded like a freight train roaring. Trees were snapping, the power went out, on and on and on. When daylight came we went out to look at our property. We had a huge oak tree in the driveway that was blown over, and several pine trees had snapped ten to fifteen feet from the ground, which indicates the tornado. But since we had no electricity, we had no pump, and therefore we had no water and had light from candles, lanterns, and flashlights. We had saved some water to drink and to bathe with.

After the third day, I needed a bath real bad. I went out to the backyard got a small bucket of water, stripped down and began to scrub my nasty body. The deal was Sylvia was going to douse me with a bucket of clean water and rinse me off when I finished. When I had been out there a short while, when I heard a vehicle come into the driveway. It was my neighbor seeing if we were okay.

There I was in the backyard with no clothes on with soap all over me. Sylvia ran out and rinsed me off real quick. I dried off with a towel and some clothes on and went out to meet my neighbor. The power was back on but the pump would not work. He said we were going to have to prime it. He helped me, and we got it started. We had no damage to the house and minor damage to my dog kennels. We had survived our first hurricane.

Some of my employees had major damage to their homes. I received a call from the home office in Birmingham, Alabama, that Mr. Charlie Clayton was coming to visit us. Mr. Clayton was about the finest man I had ever known. He showed up and brought with him some relief for our agents.

Liberty National had put a call out to all its employees to help some of the victims on the coast. One payroll week they signed up to have a deduction from our paychecks. The company matched all these funds and Mr. Clayton had the money. He called the agency and one by one discussed in detail employee damages and their problems. He made them all whole again.

I thought this was the most wonderful thing a company could do for its employees. Liberty National was always doing things like this for its employees, was a great company at one time.

Johnny's Birthday Present

Johnny would soon be heading off to school at Mississippi State and Sylvia and I thought he might need a vehicle because he wanted to come home every weekend to spend time with Sharon. So I had gone to the Ford place to pick out a nice brand-new Ford pickup truck, dark blue.

Sylvia and I wanted to surprise him so we drove the truck home and parked it in the backyard so you could not see it from the road. I told his friend Ricky to keep him on the coast that afternoon as late as he could. Sylvia and I went out and put a big ribbon all the way through the cab and tied a big bow on it with a big sign on it said "happy birthday son." In the meantime I told Johnny I wanted him home early, knowing good and well that Ricky was going to try to keep him out as long as possible.

About five thirty they arrived at home and I proceeded to complain to both of them for being so late just to throw them off guard. They both apologized I said, "Well I guess it's okay. Your mother and I talked about getting you a car so you could come home and see Sharon while you're at school." Sylvia took his hand walked to the back door, opened it, and said, "Happy birthday." I don't think I had ever seen him so excited and happy.

He got in the truck with Ricky, started it up, and drove it around in the front, turned the key off and then just looked at. We lived in an area that had a big five-to-six-mile circle on a dirt road. That evening Ricky and Johnny spent the night driving around the circle.

Sylvia and I were getting ready to go to bed and as we closed the door to the bedroom, we heard Ricky say, "Johnny, I'm not driving around that circle one more time. I'm going to bed. He took awfully good care of that truck.

He had a tendency when he drove to not tie up his tennis shoes and to kick them off and drive barefoot. One night after leaving Sharon's house, he was coming home and he kicked off one of his tennis shoes and a shoelace caught on the clutch. He leaned over to get the tennis shoe and pulled his truck to the left. There was a large drainage ditch that caught the front wheel and pulled the truck into the ditch.

At about one o'clock in the morning, he hadn't come home and I was getting concerned. The telephone rang and it was Lewis, Sharon's daddy. He said he was at the emergency room with Johnny but he was okay. Sylvia and I got dressed and headed to the coast. By the time we arrived he had been dismissed from the hospital and was at Sharon's house. He was banged up pretty good around the face but he had no broken bones or any major injuries.

They had towed his truck to the body shop. He was pretty upset and after a while I said we'd better go home. I thanked Lewis for looking after him and we headed to the house. As we drove out of the yard he said he wanted to go see his truck. I said okay and drove him by the body shop. He took one look at it and said, "Oh my goodness, my beautiful truck." Well we got it fixed and he drove her the long time back and forth from school.

PART 6
CHANGES

CHAPTER 16

Troy, Alabama

We were told that Sylvia's mother, Catherine, was diagnosed with cancer. I contacted the home office and asked him if there was anyplace close by where I could be transferred so we could look after Sylvia's mother. In a very short time there was an opening in Troy, Alabama. The district manager was retiring after thirty years. Troy was much closer, and we were glad to take that transfer. Johnny was attending Mississippi State, and soon to be married and graduate from college. So that did not create a problem.

Johnny helped us move, and I hoped he would and stay with us for the summer and help around the house. We found a place way out in the country with several acres of land, fenced and private. I had to fix a place for the bird dogs and all our other belongings.

The home we bought was in Pine Level, Alabama, about ten miles from Troy. I bought the home from a retired Air Force nurse. She had built this house, cleared a place for it at the end of a self-built road on twenty-five acres of land. It was beautiful out there. She loved animals, especially horses. She was going to give me a beautiful horse if I would take care of it. I said sure so while Johnny was staying with us, we repaired our fence in the backyard which was about one acre, and we started to put up a pole barn.

I built some dog kennels inside the fence and I acquired the horse named Dawn. This horse had been in the severe automobile accident and suffered a lot of trauma. She had some minor scarring but was a beautiful chestnut. She was extremely fractious and kinda mean. Having never been around horses much I was very cautious.

After about five days, on Friday evening Johnny came in and sat down for supper. He asked if I would loan him $50. I said sure and asked what he wanted it for. He said he wanted to go back to Long Beach so he could be near Sharon. Saturday morning he packed up his belongings with his $50 and headed to Long Beach, Mississippi.

This move by my son showed what kind of moxie he really had. He called me Monday night and said he had a place to stay, and it was in a small house behind Bruce Roberts, a classmate of his. Bruce's daddy told him that if he cleaned it up he could stay there the rest of the summer and pay $100 a month rent.

Tuesday morning he called me and said he had a job. So in a short period of time he had found a place to live and a job, and he never looked back. As soon as he got a paycheck, he sent me the $50 back. He worked all summer, went back to school, and he and Sharon were married shortly. He worked very hard in college and finished in three and a half years. He definitely had a purpose in life and was working hard to fulfill that purpose. I was so proud of him. Sharon and Johnny really worked together all of their lives.

Living in Troy was a different lifestyle than on the Gulf Coast. This was real country living. The twenty-five acres of land had only been cleared for the building of a pasture and the house; the rest of it was grown up with plenty of wild game. It had a main gate up on the highway, which you could close, and the property was completely fenced in. It was about a mile and a half down to the house.

The wild turkeys used to come and dust themselves on the dirt road in front of the house. There were all kinds of wild game there: deer, beaver, rabbits, quail, raccoons, anything you see in the wilderness.

Soon the retired Air Force nurse saw how well Dawn was doing and she would come visit me quite often and said she had another horse she wanted to give me. It was a big white gelding, seventeen and a half hands. This horse was gentle and one I could ride. And I did so frequently.

Our place in Pine Level was really wild and down the road from the highway. One Sunday I had drove up to the little country store to buy some eggs. I closed the gate behind me and started down the dirt road towards the backside where the house was located. It was a beautiful sunny day, kinda cool but nice and it was around lunchtime.

I had bought a six pack at the store and was sipping on a beer, and decided to just stop about halfway down the road, shut the car off and just sit there for a few minutes. I did, and pretty soon I saw the most beautiful stag buck deer I had ever seen. This was a granddaddy of them all he had a large rack and was very big. He came up out of the creek and looked all around. The car was not moving and neither was I. He came into the full view walked a few yards, and then went back down the creek.

I never saw him again and I sure hope nobody else saw him so he would not be shot. A few days later I was telling the boys at the store about seeing a deer. They confirmed that he was around there and had been for years but no one had been able to kill him, thank goodness. I think the word to describe him would just be majestic.

Sylvia Training Bird Dogs

I was trying to teach a dog how to hold on point when he found the bird. I had a leash about ten feet long attached to his collar and planted some birds so he could find them fairly quickly. Sylvia was going to help me that day. I told her to take a hold of the long cord and hang on tight when I flushed the bird so the dog would not chase it. She said okay.

I never realized how strong the dog was because when I flushed the bird, he started to take off. Sylvia was hanging on for dear life but the dog kept running and pulling her. I finally got ahold of the cord and stopped the dog, and that was the end of Sylvia's assistance to my training the dog.

Getting Shot At

I had asked permission from one of the farmers who had several acres of cultivated land about five or six miles from our house. I said I wanted to go bird hunting with my son down there, and he said that would be fine just as long as we made sure to close the gate on our way out. I said okay so one morning early, Johnny and I took Cindy and headed down to the man's land to hunt some quail. We hunted all morning long, and had pretty good luck.

As we were leaving and I was closing the gate we heard two rifle shots fairly close to us. It scared the hell out of both of us, and we got out of there as fast as we could. I later found out that it was one of the other neighbors who was mad about hunting on his other fellow's property. I found that he was also the driver of the Blossman Gas truck.

He pulled into my yard several days later. I reached up and jerked him right out of the car and threw him on the ground. I told him if he ever took another shot or tried to harm my family in any way I'd beat him to death, and I meant every word of it. I never heard another word from him, but we never went hunting again down there.

Puppies Being Born

It was wintertime, and I had fixed a pallet in the garage so my little bird dog could have her puppies. She began to show signs of labor and finally lay on the pallet and I watched puppies being born. There were seven of them. They were so tiny they could barely move but somehow they could crawl to her breasts to nurse. I noticed one of the puppies was being nudged by her off the pallet. I couldn't understand why she wouldn't let this puppy nurse. I guess mothers know when something's wrong with their puppies. This little pup had tried several times to crawl back onto the pallet but she would refuse him and in just a little while he stopped moving and died. The other six were all doing fine and nursing very well. All of them lived and were good, healthy bird dogs.

Comfortable Life

The prestige and reputation of Liberty National Insurance over the years had built up substantially in Troy. This was such an old established district there wasn't much to manage there as everything was in fine order. The biggest problem I had was that the Troy district had never been a leader. The agents were all pretty settled and made a good living and were pretty much satisfied with the status quo.

I had never been around an atmosphere like that and it was very difficult for me to move this district into a top-notch leadership operation. They were so set in their ways and the community was so laid-back. For example Wednesday afternoons the whole town would shut down and people would take a siesta, I guess, like they did in Mexico.

Sylvia had opened a nice bookstore in downtown Troy and because of her past experience in the book business she began to do very well. I started playing golf on Wednesday afternoons at the country club with some of the local businesspeople. This is not a lifestyle that I was used to, and I could see that I might fall into the same trap of being satisfied with mediocrity.

Sylvia and I decided we needed to move her mother and father closer to us. So we investigated the idea of maybe putting a trailer next door to us. This would be quite an ordeal because there was no way to get a big trailer down the road and across the wooden bridge. So I asked my neighbor to open his fence to let the trailer come through his property on onto our land. It was a brand-new beautiful trailer and soon Catherine and Hinton moved in. Catherine continued her cancer treatment was doing pretty good. Things seem to be settling down and getting in a regular routine.

Betting on Buck

Buck was my favorite bird dog. I had taught him how to retrieve dead birds, and he had a terrific nose. I had worked with him with a tennis ball, and would hide it in various places on the property, and would say, "Find the dead bird, Buck." He could always find it, no matter where I hid it.

One day one of my wife's friends Eleanor and her husband Alan were visiting us. He asked me about Buck, and I told him he probably had the best smeller of any dog I'd ever seen. I told him about the tennis ball. He said, "I bet I can hide it in the backyard where he can't find it." So we made a five-dollar bet. I took Buck around to the front and waited for Alan to hide the tennis ball. When he said he was ready, I turned Buck loose and told him to find the dead bird.

He searched for the tennis ball. It was amazing to watch him keep cutting the area smaller and smaller. He finally nailed it. Alan had hidden the tennis ball in the crotch of a tree thinking he could fool the dog. So I won the bet.

Riding Dawn

I had decided to try to ride Dawn, so I saddled her up, tied her to the fence post by the gate and proceeded to get on. I had a western saddle and I was throwing my right leg over the top of it. I didn't quite clear the saddle. She must've sensed I was very unsure and before I could get a good substantial seat in the saddle, she started bucking.

I was so close to the barbed wire fence and I was scared she was going to throw me right into it. I had put my hands out towards the fence to keep myself from falling into it, and that one last buck sent me up in the air and I landed right on my butt. She took off running through the pasture.

I hit so hard I must've passed out for a few minutes. I was in horrible pain and could not get up. I thought I might have broken my back so I opened the gate and had to crawl on my hands and knees to get to the back door of the house. Sylvia and her mother were in there visiting and thought I was pulling some kind of a joke.

When they realized how seriously I was hurt, they loaded me in the car and took me to the emergency room. I don't believe I had ever been in as much pain. After x-raying my back and checking me over, they could find no broken bones. The doctor told me I would be sore for a pretty good while but he didn't think I had any permanent injury.

So they drove me back home and I took pain meds for about two days. On the third day my butt turned dark purple. My whole backside had been bruised badly. I had a lot of numbness in my lower back for a long time. Even today at age eighty-three when I sit for a long time I seem to have a lot of numbness in that area. Sylvia's daddy unsaddled the horse to turn her loose. So much for my activities during that episode.

Johnny's Friend

Johnny had a friend in high school and also in college that he brought home one weekend. They wanted to go squirrel hunting. We had all kind of game so that was no problem. They arrived Friday evening around suppertime. We had supper and visited a while, and Johnny decided to take his friend down to the creek that evening late.

With flashlights at about ten o'clock that night they walked down about 100 yards from the bridge where there was a big pool of water the beaver had dammed up. I think they might have had a six pack with them but I wasn't sure. They sat on the bank and just listened.

His friend had never been in the country before and was a little bit nervous about all the racket that was going on in the woods at night. All of a sudden a large bang sounded. Several more followed. His friend was scared to death and told Johnny they'd better get back to the house. The sound was the beaver playing in the pool of water and slapping their tails, making this loud banging sound.

I don't think they went out at night on Saturday night. I think they just went squirrel hunting in the daytime. Johnny thought this was quite a funny thing. On Sunday the boys went back to school and it was good to see Johnny.

CHAPTER 17

Trying Something New

I had become more involved in the bird dogs and was spending a lot of time away from the district office. I guess I just lost interest in trying to motivate my folks to a higher level. So eventually I looked for something else to do. Liberty National was so good to me all those years, but they weren't going to put up with me not doing my job. So we parted company and I got the bright idea that I could survive in the feed business.

Johnny's major was in agriculture, and I envisioned maybe someday he and I could go into business. This was some pipedream, so I contacted the Purina company and established a working relationship with them. I rented an empty building and converted it into a feed store.

I didn't know the first thing about going into business, but I had a good idea. I knew that if I could deliver feed to the farmers in bulk, I could probably make some good money. So I invested $25,000 and bought a bulk truck.

I used to drive to Montgomery, Alabama, pick up the feed, and deliver it to the farmers. They would pay me upon delivery. I would have to pay Purina upfront and make my profit on delivery. The economic situation at this time was very bad. My inexperience combined with the interest rate of eighteen percent was not conducive to success. My first indication of a bad problem was when I delivered the feed and the farmers could not pay me. It didn't take long before I was in deep trouble.

Purina Trip

I had established a relationship with Purina, and the company had brought me to St. Louis for training. While we were there, the owner of the hockey team made his box available to us to watch the game. Previous to the game we'd had a nice steak supper. I thought this might be my last supper because I had a bone from my spareribs lodge in my throat and I could not get it out. I could not reach it with my fingers, I could not vomit it out, and I thought, "I'm going to choke to death right here."

I got a big chunk of bread and tried to swallow it. I finally had to drink a lot of water to soften the bread for it to go down but the bone would not move and I was getting very scared. I was in the bathroom stall, trying to heave it up and I finally got a hold it with my fingers and pulled it out. It was a good size bone and I kept it as a souvenir for a long time. It was surely a scary moment. I never liked being sick or having any health problems away from home all my life.

The Mill

I had put together what I thought was a good business plan. I was going to construct this large building to make my own feed. This was about a $1 million project and required a lot of support from the community. Plus I needed investors, and I spent a lot of time trying to put this together.

For various reasons it failed to materialize, and I finally had to file bankruptcy. I had a lot of obligations and no money coming in. Sylvia's bookstore was doing well enough to produce grocery money but that was about it. So I lost everything but my automobile. We had to move Sylvia's mother and daddy back to Phenix City, I lost the house, and we had to move back too. I had no job, no money, and plenty of obligations left.

So my only choice was to turn back to the insurance business. I was burned out on all that, but I knew that was the only thing I could do. So I took a couple of jobs and made a little money while looking

for something better. Johnny in the meantime had got married and
he and Sharon were toughing it out at school. Thank God he didn't
have to go through any of this.

Full-Time Job

One of my old friends who had worked with Liberty National had
taken a job as vice president of a small insurance company. He called
me and asked me if I would go to work for them being a trouble-
shooter. I didn't really care what I was doing as long as I had some
money coming in. So I had to travel. This company had districts all
over Alabama, and my job was to go there and make sure everything
was running smoothly. They furnished an automobile and an ex-
pense account.

Sylvia and I in the meantime had moved in to the old house
at 4302 Somerville Road in Phenix City, Alabama. I stayed on the
road five days a week, lived in a motel, and we got paid every Friday.
Sylvia managed the money and kept us afloat. Since I had filed bankruptcy I did not have a checking account or any credit. So everything
we did was on a cash basis. I did this for a short period of time and
gave us a little breathing room.

My friend had a severe heart attack and was no longer able to do
his job. The company offered me a manager's job at the nearby town
of Opelika, Alabama. I gladly accepted because it meant more money and I could be home every day. So I took the job, and we started
to do a little better.

CHAPTER 18

Added Responsibilities

Sylvia's daddy had passed away, and her mother was completely bed-ridden. She needed care twenty-four/seven. Her uncle, who was almost totally blind, had a wife who suddenly became a dialysis patient. She had an aunt in an assisted living home in South Georgia. All of a sudden, all these folks were Sylvia's and my responsibility. Dialysis three times a week, twice a month visits to South Georgia, grocery buying for her uncle. Catherine needed constant care. We were full of obligations and we try to manage the best we could with it.

We managed to get her aunt in South Georgia moved to Opelika into a nursing home. She wasn't very well but she was close to us. This routine went on for several months and put a lot of stress on Sylvia. I could at least go to work every day, but she had to stay at home with her mother and worry about these other relatives.

Her aunt in the nursing home was the first to pass away. Shortly afterward, her second aunt who was on dialysis passed away. Then in a few months her mother passed away. That left her uncle who was almost blind to care for.

Sylvia and I both wanted to go back to the coast. So I put out some feelers and got a job, and we moved back to the coast. In the meantime her uncle was living alone in Phenix City with a lot of help from us making sure he was okay. The day we were going to move back to the coast I called Bubba, her uncle, and said we were going back to the coast. That night he called me back, and said he wanted to go with us. We weren't prepared for this, but we managed and moved back to the coast.

The job I had was a good one, and the company had some good products to sell. I began to do very well and was making decent money. I still had three dogs left our pet. Our big great Pyrenees Roxie, Duchess, and Buck my bird-dog. So there we were, Sylvia, me, the dogs and Bubba. We were doing okay.

We used to go shopping for groceries with Bubba and he was so set in his ways that he would buy only brand name products that he had used for years. He was so blind he could not read any labels so it was quite an ordeal. He always paid his way and was really not a big problem. Duchess got hit by a car. Soon Bubba was hospitalized and passed away in the hospital.

There we were, just me and Sylvia. We really didn't know what to do, but we were relieved of the pressure. So we adjusted and I continued to work for the company.

Change in Products

The company that I had worked for all of a sudden dropped one of their best sellers where I had made the most money. So my sales began to drop considerably. In the months ahead they lost their competitive edge, and I lost my market. So I had to move on.

Sylvia and the meantime had opened up a bookstore in Long Beach, Mississippi, and was trying to get off to a good start. I helped her out in the bookstore is much as I could but still kept looking for a decent job. I was getting so depressed I remember sitting in her bookstore one day just crying.

We had moved across the street from our old friends Rex and Jean. I developed a medical problem that required surgery and put me where I could not work for about four weeks.

Finally I was looking around for job and saw an ad in the local paper for job I thought I might could do. I interviewed for this job and was hired.

New Job

My new job was to obtain Medicaid for people who had no insurance and had large medical bills from all types of providers, mostly hospitals. These providers were anxious for the persons to obtain Medicaid so they could qualify for a Medicaid number. When receiving this number, the providers could file a claim on that number and receive some type of payment on the bill.

This method was a good idea, and if my company obtained any payment to the provider, the provider would pay a percentage of that amount to my company. The job was new to me but my background dealing with people in the medical field was very useful. I soon got the hang of it and was doing pretty good. I had a regular paycheck, good working conditions, and a captive source.

There was a lawyer in the same office building where I was who did disability representation. He suggested that I should learn to represent my clients in hearings so they could qualify for disability and get SSI (Supplemental Security Income). He helped me get started and gave me lots of good pointers and I had my first hearing.

To say the least I was very nervous, but the judge I had was extremely nice to me and knew this was my first hearing. He guided me through what I should do and what I should not do in the future, which helped me a lot. I continued to work hard on Medicaid disability for my company and tried to develop my expertise doing disability hearings.

I soon found out that the money was going to be in the disability representation and that my company was never going to pay me what I was worth, so I decided to develop my expertise even further. The company I worked for didn't seem to be interested at all in any direction of disability, only with Medicaid. So Sylvia and I talked about it, and I decided to go it alone and open my own business, just disability representation. I turned my resignation in and started my own business

170

First Payday

I had rented a small office in a nice office building not too far from where I already worked. My first paycheck from disability was around $8,000 which took care of my business expenses for the first couple of months. When Sylvia and I went to the post office that Saturday morning and I got that check, she and I were both excited.

I furnished my office with some moderate furniture and hired a part-time secretary. This lady I hired had had a lot of experience in the Medicaid business and was quite helpful. The biggest problem with the operation was collecting the money. Not being an attorney I was not allowed to have my fees withheld from the claimant's settlement. We had to be right on top of that so when they received their disability check, we could get our money that day.

The majority of the clients I did disability for had no checking account and no credit. And when they received a large check from Social Security, they were unable to cash it. I had had a good relationship with one of the local banks and was able to take my clients to the bank so they could cash their checks. They would in turn pay me the same day they cashed the check and that seemed to solve the problem temporarily. I had adequate savings in my bank account, so the bank didn't mind cashing the checks for them.

I had a nice new office on the second floor of an office building downtown and eventually extended my office to cover the whole suite of five rooms. I eventually was able to hire five ladies to do the job. As an extra incentive I used to give them a bonus if they could get a Medicaid number prior to my taking a client to the hearing. They all worked hard to get the extra money. The business was really doing well and we were all working hard and having a good time.

Disruptive Client

In one of my hearings in Gulfport, Mississippi, I had a young lady who was trying to get on disability but didn't have much of a case. I had to take it because it was assigned to me from the hospital. When we got before the judge, who was very thorough and asked the client a lot of questions, she began to get trapped in several lies.

The longer the hearing went on, the madder she got. She finally jumped up out of her chair and laid a real crescendo of curse words on me and the judge, and said, "What the hell am I doing in here anyway?" She was very vocal and you could hear her all over the waiting room. She stormed out of the hearing, slammed the door and left the building.

The judge very calmly said, "I think she might've got a little bit upset." When I left the hearing room and went out into the waiting area, there were several people waiting for the hearing. Some of the representatives that I knew well said, "John you need to have better control of your client."

Personal Life

We had bought a house in Long Beach, Mississippi, and had it completely remodeled and refurnished. We built a beautiful courtyard in back of the house and put stamped concrete designs all over the backyard. I put a nice hot tub in there and had some beautiful flowers, and it really looked nice. I built two large outbuildings in the back of the house, one for a workshop and one for an exercise room. The workshop contained all the things the workshop should, and the exercise room was top-notch. It had a really nice treadmill and an exercise machine called a Nu Step, air conditioning, hardwood floors, and an exercise bar on the wall. I used to work out regularly, and it did me some good. We were living pretty good.

Unfortunately, I had talked Sylvia into taking her broker's license, even though she didn't want to. I think the pressure just got to be too much for her. One day she called me and was mumbling incoherently. I went home and found her in bed. She had had small stroke.

Trip to Vermont

I managed to take all three of my grandchildren to Vermont, where I was born and raised. John had three children: Michael, Lauren and Nicole. We had a two-week vacation and stayed right on Lake Rescue, and the children had a wonderful time. In conjunction with this I had talked to Johnny and Sharon about taking a vacation themselves. So I set up a vacation to Jamaica for them while we were in Vermont.

The children really enjoyed it, and so did Sylvia and I. There was plenty of fishing, swimming, boating, and meeting a lot of new people. One of the most fascinating things about this trip was everyone wanted to hear my grandchildren speak. They all had that good old southern drawl and welcomed the chance to talk to everybody.

There was an island several hundred yards from our cabin. Michael and Lauren would swim out there and spent a lot of time. They had made some friends who were from the city vacationing at Lake Rescue. We had a kayak underneath the porch at the cabin and Lauren became pretty good at maneuvering it around. I later found out that Michael had gone tubing with some of his new friends.

Nicole could sit on the dock and catch those great big bass and hold them up so the bass fisherman would see them. They were in bass boats further out in the lake. They had all the equipment necessary to catch fish. Nicole didn't have anything but a rod and worms.

One evening we invited my brother Bruce to come have supper with us. Sylvia cooked a real good meal, and he came and visited with us a long time. We later got to see his beautiful home on top of the mountain, which was truly gorgeous.

This trip was one week before 9/11. We had landed in Boston and taken a smaller airplane to Rutland Vermont.

The children saw all of the Green Mountain sights and beautiful lakes and really enjoyed themselves.

I wanted to go to Lake Ninevah. I really wanted to see if the steppingstone was still in place at the cabin. I talked about it earlier in my memoirs when my granddad and I had worked so hard to put it

The slab stone in front of the cabin.
Taken July 2019.

there. So I took the car and drove up to the cabin.

When I arrived, there were some young people staying at the cabin. I walked over to the door, and sure enough the slab was still in place. I stomped on it several times, and began to tear up a lot. That marble slab had so many memories of my youth with my grandparents.

We all had a good time except for the last day. Sylvia had slipped on the stairway and injured her foot. We had no way of knowing at the time that she had broken some bones, and she did not complain too much. But this turned out to be a major problem. She had broken the outside bone in her right foot, and walked around all over the airport and on the way back home.

She began having a lot of pain, and went to an orthopedic doctor in Gulfport, Mississippi. This was not a good move at all. The doctor was not doing her any good and wanted to put her on pain medication. She wouldn't go for that, so we made an appointment with a specialist in New Orleans, Louisiana. His son used to work in Gulfport as an orthopedic surgeon and this doctor was highly respected. He took some x-rays of Sylvia's foot and found the problem. He put her in the boot, and she had to wear that boot for a long time with several trips to New Orleans. Eventually it healed and she was okay.

Nicole

When we had the children visit us, once late at night, Nicole woke me up and she said she was very sick. She was running a little fever. I guess she didn't want to wake up her mom and daddy, so she came to me. I got a blanket and a little ginger ale, and held her on my chest in my big recliner. After a while, she looked up at me and said and said, "Paw Paw, would you watch over me?" I said, "Yes, I'll watch over you." Later, I would pretend to be sick and she would be Nurse Carrie.

Michael

I had a Chevrolet pickup truck, and when my grandson Michael was with us, he was determined to get me to teach them how to drive. I would not let him drive out in the street. He drove the pickup truck up and down the driveway, until he said, "When can I drive it on the road?" I told him not yet.

Red Christmas Presents

Every Christmas Eve we would shop when Sylvia was able and we would take all our presents to Johnny's house in Madison, Mississippi. I had a white El Dorado Cadillac with a large trunk. That Christmas all the Christmas presents were wrapped with red paper, and the back seat was full as well as a trunk. We were really looking forward to spending Christmas with Johnny and Sharon and their children.

About twenty-five miles from Jackson, I had a flat tire. I had pulled into the middle of the four-lane road and started to unload all the presents to get to the spare tire. Well I had them all stacked up on the side of the road and Sylvia was sitting in a lawn chair watching me. When I got the spare tire out it was flat. It was Christmas Eve and I was in a hell of a fix. This nice young man pulled off the road next to my car to help. He said there was a place up the road where I might get some air in my spare tire.

Now I did a very foolish thing and left Sylvia sitting on the side of the road with all those presents and went off with this man I had never met to get some air for my tire. I wasn't really thinking about Sylvia's safety; I was thinking about getting to Johnny's. Fortunately for us a highway patrolman came by and saw Sylvia sitting in the chair with all red presents and asked her where her husband was.

She said, "He's gone to get some air for our spare tire."

He said, "Ma'am, you don't need to be sitting out here all by yourself. So he waited and watched over her until I got back. This was surely a nice thing for him to do and I thanked him profusely.

CHAPTER 19

Kiln, Mississippi

A couple of years later, Sylvia and I decided we might take a vacation by ourselves. We wanted to go somewhere kind of private that had some country surroundings, not near the beach. So we went to the Smokies. It was anything but private; there were tourists everywhere. Even the chalet we had rented was crowded.

We were very disappointed in that part of our trip. I had wanted to go fishing, and found the lake somewhere out in the wilderness. I finally found the lake, rented a boat and motor and fished without success for about five hours.

I had done a pretty stupid thing. I left Sylvia at the cabin by herself with no phone and no way to contact me. I could have drowned or been in an accident. The trip was nothing like we had expected. We spent too much money and did not have a good time.

On our way back, we had talked about maybe finding a place somewhere about twenty-five or thirty miles from the coast that we could go on weekends and maybe escape from a hurricane. We looked around and finally located a small house and five acres of land in Kiln, Mississippi. Sylvia looked at this little house and could see a lot of potential. I didn't see any of that.

I contacted Joe, who had been a wonder remodeling our house in Long Beach, and asked him to meet me up at the house. After some discussion, Sylvia agreed on what she wanted to do to remodel this house. Joe and I agreed on a price, and I gave him the cash to start the project. Every Friday we would visit Joe and see with the progress he was making.

He was an honest, honorable and trustworthy man, and would give me a detailed accounting of all the money he had spent. I would pay him and we would drive back to Long Beach. We were really excited about moving in on the weekends.

Finally the house was completed and it was amazing. The best feature was an L-shaped wraparound screened-in porch. We cleared all the land off, dug a pond, and stocked it with bass and bream.

The Peacock

Early one morning I was sitting on the screened-in porch at the table, drinking a cup of coffee. I looked over to the edge of the woods saw this huge bird rambling towards the dam. I didn't know what to make of it because it was so far away. As he got closer I realized it was a large peacock. The plume on the back was quite long and the peacock was very pretty.

He was striding along slowly and every once in a while he would make his loud, shrill call. He just kept strolling along on the dirt path leading to the gate. He went out the front gate and I never saw him again.

I did find out that my neighbor a few miles away had a peacock farm and this one might have escaped and was looking to go back home. But this was something for me to witness early in the morning. I did find out later also that peacocks make really good watchdogs. They make this loud, shrill sound, which would alert you if something was amiss.

The Fishing Pole That Almost Got Away

I was fishing in our pond in the country one day, and I had a large bamboo pole and a spinning rod. I had baited the bamboo pole thinking I might catch some bream or maybe a big bass I threw it in the water as far as I could and set the pole down. I had a cooler beside my chair and reached over to get a cold beer. I had set my spinning rod down for just a few seconds, and the bamboo pole was still in the water when all of a sudden it took off.

I couldn't grab ahold of it in time and it went out through the water just lickety-split. I watched the pole swim all over the pond. Evidently what was on the end couldn't get off and was dragging the pole for several minutes. The pole finally settled on the opposite side of the pond in a marshy area.

The pole was sticking straight up in the water about three and a half feet. I got my little riding mower and lassoed the pole with clothesline. I had to tug on it pretty good because it was stuck in the mud. When I got the line out of the water, the hook was all bent out of shape and there was no fish on the end. I never knew what got ahold of that but I had stocked up the pond with some bass and I knew there were some large ones in there.

Bicycle Accident
One afternoon Sylvia and I were coming back from shopping, and I pulled out to the side street and was going very slow. All of a sudden this young boy on a bicycle crashed right into the driver's side and flew over the windshield and landed on the ground.

I told Sylvia, "I think I've killed that boy." I pulled off the road to the right, where there was a little drainage ditch. I was pulled so far to the right that Sylvia could not get out through her car door. I managed to pull her out and we got out on the road.

The boy was sitting on the pavement. Our windshield was cracked, and his bicycle was destroyed. I asked him if he was okay, and he said he was fine. We called the police to the scene of the accident.

When they were doing their report, his mother and brother arrived, and she gave him a talking to in the world's worse way. She said, "I told you not to ride your bicycle in this area." Thank God he was all right and I had minor damage to the car. But it scared the daylights out of both of us.

Living in the Country
Joe, who had remodeled our house, his wife Lisa, Sylvia and I were

living in that little house in the country and going to work every day. We would stay up there and Sylvia would do all the cooking so we had a decent meal in the evening.

We were surrounded by love bugs everywhere. It was hard to keep them out of your house and keep your car clean of the bugs. Everyone had the same problem and there wasn't much we could do. Then finally one day they just disappeared. That was a real blessing.

One Friday evening, Joe, Lisa and Sylvia and I were having supper, sitting at the kitchen table. Sylvia was a good cook and we'd had a hard week. About the time the meal ended, Joe turned to me and said, "You know, Mr. B, I never thought I'd be sitting down having dinner with white folks on Friday night."

I said, "Well, Joe, that makes us even. I never thought I'd be sitting down with black folks on Friday night having supper. It's pretty good though, isn't it"

He said "It sure is."

Tragedy Strikes
On Saturday nights, Sylvia used to fix us a nice meal. She had recovered from her stroke and was doing well. She had developed Parkinson's Disease, which she inherited from her mother. She never developed tremors, but it affected her balance, making her unstable. But she could still fix meals and get around. She could be left alone and go shopping by herself.

We ate by candlelight with a bottle wine, sitting out there overlooking the pond. The only sounds you could hear were the frogs croaking. It was so peaceful and we had such good times there. My business was doing well when tragedy struck.

Sylvia had her second stroke one Sunday while we were in the country. I rushed her to the hospital. They began treatment and she stayed a couple of days. She received some kind of damage to her speech. It turned out to be aphasia. Her ability to speak was severely impaired, but everything else seemed to be intact. She took speech therapy for a while with minimal results. Her mind was still sharp, but she couldn't communicate. She never fully recovered.

I had developed a right knee meniscus tear and had to have surgery. I missed several days at work and soon found out that while the cat's away the mice to play. The business began to suffer some and then out of the blue came Hurricane Katrina.

Hurricane Katrina

This hurricane was one of the most devastating hurricanes to hit the Gulf Coast. We did not live right on the beach but were about three blocks from it. We were given plenty of warning to get out of town and make our preparations. We did not realize the severity of the storm and decided to go to the country and ride it out. Johnny insisted that we not stay there and come to Madison, Mississippi, to stay with him. So we headed up the highway bound for Madison.

This trip probably would take about three hours normally, but due to the heavy traffic leaving the coast it took us nearly eight hours to get there. It was the most nerve-racking trip, bumper-to-bumper, a few feet in a time, and very frustrating. We finally arrived at Johnny's house safe and sound and we were exhausted.

The news was not good. We stayed glued to the TV and the radio to make sure we had the proper updates. The storm finally made landfall and the devastation was beyond belief. We wanted to get back to see if our house was still intact in Long Beach, but they were not letting any people in below the railroad tracks.

Finally they opened up with a permit to cross the railroad tracks. They had armed guards all along the tracks so you couldn't get to your home without a permit. So Johnny and Sharon and I loaded up his truck with some gasoline, guns, and equipment we thought we would need to start cleaning up the house. The trip down there revealed that there was lots of damage away from the coast. The tremendous wind had knocked down trees beyond the city of Hattiesburg. The closer we got to the beach, the more we realized we might not even have a home.

When we finally arrived it was beyond belief. The first thought I had was to have the house bulldozed to the ground. We did not have flood insurance but we had a homeowners policy, as did most people in that area, and we took a real beating financially. Johnny and Sharon and I started trying to clean up inside the house. It was full of mud and water, and all the furniture was destroyed. The rugs were quite expensive, we had several, and they were soaked. Johnny and I had a hard time loading each one of them in the wheelbarrow and taking them to the front yard. There was not much left to salvage but I gathered up a few things to save.

Johnny and Sharon worked very, very hard and after a while, we decided the house was worth saving. I was able to get a new roof on the house within a week, which was a blessing. After working all day in this horrible mess and seeing the devastation, we headed back to Madison.

On our next trip, Joe and his wife Lisa were staying in the country at our little house and started on the house in Long Beach to get it back in order. We all worked very hard to try to get the place cleaned up. After a few trips down there we began to see daylight. Joe and Lisa worked every day cleaning up this awful mess. The sheet rock about thirty-six inches up all through the house had to be cut off and replaced. The flooring all had to be replaced, and Sylvia's Lincoln, which was in the driveway, was crushed. So I had to make arrangements to file a claim on my automobile insurance.

Everything was in such turmoil, people had no place to live and very few supplies, and there was total chaos for several days. Slowly things began to look up and take shape. In the meantime I had gone downtown to my office to see what was left. It was on the second floor not far from the beach in Gulfport. All the buildings in the area were totally destroyed. My office and all equipment, files, and so on were gone.

Bose Equipment

Katrina had damaged all my sound equipment. I had had several thousand dollars' worth of top-notch Bose equipment. I located a person in Gulfport, Mississippi, who could do an inventory of my loss. He knew all about the Bose equipment and he made a list of all my damage. I contacted the Bose Corporation and told them what it happened. They said to mail them a list of all my equipment that was damaged. I did so.

Within a short period of time I received all the necessary equipment to restore my Bose equipment. I cannot tell you what a wonderful company this is. There was no charge, not even the shipping. I soon had it all restored back in number one working order.

The treadmill company who made my exercise equipment did not help one bit. I still have all my Bose equipment packed up ready to use again.

Starting Over

Since the house in Long Beach was being worked on diligently every day, it was time for me to tackle what was left of my business. My secretary, Angie, had had sense enough to store all my data on computers and had taken the computer disks with her to Maryland, where she stayed with her relatives. Thank God for Angie.

I needed to find a location to reopen my office and see how to proceed. I had several hearings pending, no office, and no way to go to a hearing. The Social Security office had major damage so it was not even open.

I began looking for a small office and I found one, but it was so small and out of the way that it wasn't feasible for me to do business there. Soon the Social Security office began to put up temporary trailers and got in a position where they could resume video hearings with the help of judges everywhere. Katrina had made such a big backlog that this was a monumental task and involved planning.

I finally found an office downtown several blocks from the beach that had minor damage and had been repaired. I had to hire a new secretary, buy new equipment, and try to get started. When I was able to resume my hearing schedule, I would have five or six in one day. I remember one day I had seven hearings with a judge from Sarasota, Florida. I had never met him, knew nothing about him, but I was prepared for the hearings.

At eight o'clock that morning we started. His introduction was, "Mr. Barnard, we don't know each other, but by the end of the day we should be well acquainted." I chuckled and said, "I guess so, Judge." And we worked nonstop with about thirty minutes for lunch. Late that evening we completed all seven. This was quite a day. Life as we knew it in the past was never going to be the same. Everyone had to make substantial adjustments to survive.

Locating Clients

The majority of my disability cases had been moved all over the place. Some were in New Orleans headed for Texas, some were on a boat outside of Mobile where they had provided the cruise ship. Some were in North Carolina, and others I just couldn't find. My business had turned into a struggling small business that was not producing a lot of income. I struggled along for two months just getting by.

We were able to move back into our home in Long Beach, and Joe and Lisa had put a FEMA trailer up in the front yard of our place in the country. This was the best we could do at the time. I had depleted most of my savings trying to get back on my feet and had a real problem with cash flow. Somehow we managed to hang on for a few months and all of the coast was under real adjustments.

Tragedy Strikes Again

I noticed one morning at home I had a small knot under my right ear on my neck, right where the lymph nodes were. I went to my doctor and had it checked out and he did a biopsy. His nurse called and set up an appointment to discuss the results.

Sylvia and I were sitting in his office, and he said, "John, you have a cancer." I was shocked. I hadn't felt any symptoms of anything wrong. He proceeded to tell me the type of cancer; it was Merkel Cell. Since I had just discovered a lump on my neck, I decided the best thing to do is to get it over as quick as possible.

I called Johnny and told him about it. The next thing I knew we had made an application to the cancer center MD Anderson in Houston, Texas. Sharon had made all arrangements for us to fly out there, so John and I kept our appointment. This facility was surely if not the best one of the best in the country for treating cancer. This place was so organized it was unbelievable.

After full week of testing with every department necessary we returned home. John and I had to make one more trip. This time we had a thorough discussion and went through all the options. They said they would let me know on Friday morning what the decision was on how to proceed.

So Friday morning before we left to come home I received an email stating what they recommended and when to get started. John and I had a long discussion on the way home about that and after we arrived at home we started checking out the options.

Sylvia could not go with me and stay during my chemotherapy and radiation treatment in Houston. So my son had some kind of a relationship with a friend who got me in to see Dr. Graham at the cancer center at St. Dominic's hospital in Jackson.

All my records and the regime they wanted me to start were sent to Dr. Graham from MD Anderson. When we went to him, he had reviewed all the information and suggested we start right away. He said he could start me on chemotherapy at St. Dominic's. So Sylvia and I moved to Madison to stay with Johnny and Sharon while I took chemotherapy. Johnny drove me every day and for four the weeks I received chemotherapy.

The next step was radiation, which was done in the same location. Dr. Graham had put me in touch with Dr. Belfour, who was a radiation doctor. I was able to drive myself every day to radiation while Sylvia stayed at Johnny's house. I had forty treatments. I would have regularly scheduled follow-ups with Dr. Graham and he seemed pretty optimistic.

I had been away from my business so long there was no chance for me to recoup. So I closed my business, took all my equipment, put it in storage, and finished up what hearing cases I had, and we were faced with starting over again.

CHAPTER 20
Losing Sylvia

Move to Jackson, Mississippi

Johnny and Sharon in the meantime were really worried about me and Sylvia. She had gotten worse and needed constant supervision. Johnny said, "Daddy, you're going to have to sell your house and move to Jackson. I didn't much cotton to that idea but I knew that was probably the only answer. So through a mutual friend we put our house up for sale, and shortly it was sold. In the meantime Johnny and Sharon found us a house and purchased it. I don't know how they did everything they did, but Sylvia and I really appreciated it.

We packed all our stuff, which took the better part of two weeks. They had rented a truck with some workers and went down to move us. We had accumulated so much that the truck they hired was not near big enough to hold all of it. So John and Sharon had to go back the next day, rent a U-Haul, load it up, and head back to Jackson. We waited about three days. There were installing hardwood floors in the house, so I could get around in my wheelchair. We moved in.

Johnny and Sharon had worked so hard, especially Sharon. Inside the house everything was set up just like she thought we would want it when we moved in. The house was sold and I received my money and I paid off all my debts. I tried to talk to Johnny about paying the rent, but he wouldn't even listen to me. He said, "Daddy, don't worry about it." So here we were.

House in the Country

I had rented our house in the country to my old secretary, Kimberly

Kennedy, and still had a payment to make on it every month. After a few months, she began to fall behind on the rent and it became a real problem. Finally I had to tell her that I was going to sell house because I could not afford to keep it any longer. She had assured me she was going to try to buy the house, so I didn't worry too much about selling it. Big mistake.

No activity on her part to buy the house, so I made a decision to sell it. I gave her thirty days to move. I was about to hire the same real estate agent who sold my house in Long Beach when out of the blue one of my neighbors' daughters called me and said, "I understand you're going to sell your house." I said yes and she said she wanted to buy it.

We came to an agreement on the price, and I sold the house for cash. That saved us all a lot of money and relieved me of a tremendous burden. Now we were in our new house and for the first time in a long time I had a little savings and was not under financial pressure.

New Medical Doctors
We were fortunate enough to get referrals to all the doctors for Sylvia. Our house was located not too far from St. Dominic's hospital in Jackson, and most of the doctors' offices were in the general vicinity. We started visiting them one by one and established a doctor-patient relationship.

Sylvia was getting worse, and the Parkinson's disease was progressing. Thank God I was able to stay with her. The next two years were a living hell for both of us. I was not prepared to be a caregiver and had to learn how to do everything. I managed to learn some things pretty quick but had to call Sharon for advice on cooking. We managed and were able to get home healthcare, which helped a lot.

Sylvia had a bad problem about falling down and had fallen several times. Fortunately she did not injure herself, but it scared me half to death every time she fell. She was taking Coumadin and every time she would fall it seemed like she had to have a CAT scan to see if there was any damage to her brain. She was in the hospital for short time and didn't do well at all. Upon discharge she was glad to be home and seemed to improve somewhat.

She continued to deteriorate in all phases of her life. This was the most difficult time for me because I could not do anything to stop it, and after a few months she had a real bad fall that hurt her hip. There were no broken bones but she developed a large hematoma. She was hospitalized again and treated with a wound VAC for several days. She was not responding well at all, and my grandson Michael, who was a doctor at St. Dominic's, proceeded to help us get her on hospice care.

Hospice Care

We brought her home for little while, and she did a little better. The hospice people were extremely nice, very helpful. Her health was failing rapidly, and it was harder and harder for me to care for her. I had finally moved her from her hospital bed in the front room to our bed. I had to tie a bathrobe sash to her leg and the other to my leg so she could not get out of bed at night without me knowing it. It was so hard for her and me.

On October 22, early in the morning, Sylvia had a massive stroke, and fell. She never did regain consciousness and was in a bad way. The hospice people came right away when I called them in. My grandson Michael came also. She started having seizures one right after another, and I could not watch them. I had seen little Michael several years ago do the same thing. About two o'clock that after-noon, we decided it was time to take her to the hospice facility as I could no longer care for her.

They came and took her by ambulance and we followed shortly behind. The seizures had ceased but she was still unconscious. They took her to her room and told us we could see her later on that af-ternoon. So John and I came home, and later that evening we went to see her. She was quietly resting in the bed, totally unaware of her surroundings and I knew this was going to be the end soon.

Johnny left the room, and I leaned over and kissed her and said, "Baby, I love you. That was the last time I saw my lovely wife.

We then came home and at five fifteen the next morning they called me and told me she had passed away. We had made arrangements to have her cremated and her ashes be buried next to our other two children in Phenix City, Alabama. This was a sad day for all of us. Sylvia and I would have been married sixty years on December 27, 2018. For fifty-nine and a half years we had been together and shared some wonderful moments. We had some bad times just like any couple. But she was always there with me and for me.

I know now that she is resting peacefully and is a much better place. Sylvia was a tough customer and would not give up. I know that trait is embedded in my son John and hopefully my grandchildren.

We had her funeral at Lakeview Memory Gardens in November. I rode with Johnny. Michael and his wife Olivia were able to come also. Sylvia's oldest friend Eleanor and her two children who grew up with Johnny were also in attendance. We had a simple graveside service, which was what we both discussed and what she wanted. Her brother Danny was also there.

Loneliness

It will soon be a year since Sylvia passed away. It's so lonely without her and I miss her so much. I knew I could not sit here and do nothing so I decided to write an autobiography. I still have my little pet kitty cat named Prissy. She came to us right after Hurricane Katrina in 2005. She truly loved Sylvia and Sylvia loved her. She has been slow to warm up to me, but now she follows me everywhere and has become very lovable.

I would be remiss at this stage to not talk about my neighbors. Rosemary and her daughter April were a godsend to us. Rosemary is a registered nurse, and her daughter April is always there for us. They were so helpful with Sylvia and now they check on me regularly.

My son Johnny checks with me every day and I'm so thankful I still have him.

He has been through so much this past year as well. His lovely wife Sharon suddenly passed away at age fifty-five. His mother passed away eight months later and he's had cancer surgery, plus he has just been promoted to a very important job. He finished purchasing the new house with a gorgeous swimming pool that he and Sharon had already set in motion. He has really had to cope with a lot of tragedy this past year and a half.

Recently he has made contact with a lovely lady from Louisiana. He seems to have some sort of the purpose and maybe something will come of it. Don't know, but if it does it does.

Moving On
I will soon have my eighty-fourth birthday, and I'm trying to move on. I managed to make a trip to Vermont to visit old friends to stay with my brother this summer. The trip rejuvenated me and I was able to close the book on several questions I had regarding the Lake Nineveh property.

I had a wonderful time and had forgotten how beautiful Vermont really is. I'm hoping now that my new goal will help me get my writings published and someone will enjoy reading them. This will take some time as I now need to find an editor, a publisher, and the market. I'm looking forward to the challenge which will keep me busy for quite some time.

Made in the USA
Columbia, SC
15 June 2020